The inspiring story of a strong man who became even stronger in the Lord.

"I had driven the 414½ pounds overhead and had won the gold medal — the last United States heavyweight lifter to do so, as it has turned out. I had lifted far more in the past and would lift much more in the future. The poundage was not important. Even the gold medal was not the real prize. A far greater miracle had occurred. What I really won was not an Olympic championship measured by the poundages of man but the strength of God's Holy Spirit. I had finally learned that His strength would not be diluted by the diseases of my vulnerable flesh-and-bone structure."

In these pages, Paul Anderson tells how he discovered a *greater strength* through Christ, which enables him to flourish in his outreach and remain faithful through difficult times. Now, instead of lifting weights, Paul Anderson lifts up people's hearts to the Lord. Is adversity draining your strength? *A Greater Strength* will encourage you to persevere as it testifies to the promise that "those who hope in the Lord will renew their strength" (Isaiah 40:31a NIV).

A Greater Strength

A Greater Strength

Paul Anderson
with
Jerry B. Jenkins and James R. Adair

Power Books
Fleming H. Revell Company
Old Tappan, New Jersey

Unless otherwise identified, Scripture quotations are from the King James Version of the Bible.

Scripture verses marked TLB are taken from *The Living Bible,* Copyright © 1971 by Tyndale House Publishers, Wheaton, Ill. Used by permission.

This is an expanded, updated edition of *The World's Strongest Man.*

Material from *SUPER SQUATS: How to Gain 30 Pounds of Muscle in 6 Weeks* by Randall J. Strossen, Ph.D., is reprinted by permission of the publisher, IronMind™ Enterprises, Larkspur, California.

Quotation from the *Guinness Book of World Records,* published by Guinness Publishing, copyright © Guinness Publishing Limited 1989.

Excerpts from story in March 10, 1990, issue of the *Augusta Chronicle* used by permission of the *Augusta Chronicle.*

Material from *The New York Times* copyright © 1956 by The New York Times Company. Reprinted by permission.

Quotation from the March 20, 1990, issue of the *Times,* Gainesville, Georgia, used by permission.

Library of Congress Cataloging-in-Publication Data

Anderson, Paul.
    A greater strength / Paul Anderson with Jerry B. Jenkins and James R. Adair.
        p.   cm.
    Expanded ed. of: The world's strongest man. © 1975.
    ISBN 0-8007-5366-6
    1. Anderson, Paul. 2. Weightlifters—United States—Biography. 3. Weightlifters—United States—Religious life—Case studies. I. Jenkins, Jerry B. II. Adair, James R.
III. Anderson, Paul. World's strongest man. IV. Title.
GV545.52.A53A3   1990
796.41′092—dc20   90-33823
[B]   CIP

Copyright © 1975 by SP Publications, Inc.; 1990 by Paul Anderson
Published by the Fleming H. Revell Company
Old Tappan, New Jersey 07675
Printed in the United States of America

To all of the faithful supporters who have stood by
Glenda and me as we have ministered to our boys at the
Paul Anderson Youth Home

Contents

Foreword

Annually, many interesting autobiographies are written by achievers, but few are by people who have completely dominated in their fields. Only these people become legends.

In the sports world, when a champion of one era is compared with a champion of another era, the inevitable conclusion is that "the old-timers were great in their day, but compared with today's champions, there is no comparison." However true this statement is, history will, in a rare moment, produce a champion who is so gifted that he will completely dominate his field. Paul Anderson is one of those champions.

Paul's accomplishments in the weightlifting field may even surpass many other legendary records such as Byron Nelson's 11 consecutive golf tournament wins or Cy Young's pitching record of 511 victories. To be included in this unique group of champions, an athlete must be able to completely "shatter the confidence" of his opponents. Paul Anderson was able to do this by breaking existent records, not by two or three pounds but sometimes by hundreds of pounds.

My friendship with Paul Anderson began in the early years of my coaching career, growing out of our mutual interest in the

Fellowship of Christian Athletes and our work together on its board of trustees.

As much as you will enjoy reading about the rise of Paul Anderson to superstar status, I believe you will discover, as I have, an extraordinary man whom God has used to lift more than steel. Since 1961 he and his wife, Glenda, have been caring, loving parents to hundreds of troubled young people, supplying the boost they need to turn their lives around. Remarkably, despite severe health struggles for the past decade, Paul, with the steadfast support of Glenda, has continued to direct the life-changing ministry from a wheelchair. Thus, more than ever now, "The World's Strongest Man" relies daily on spiritual strength from Jesus Christ, to whom he committed himself as he captured the Gold during the 1956 Olympics.

Tom Landry, Head Coach,
Dallas Cowboys, 1960–1989

Introduction
Why This Book?

For years I had been making numerous public appearances giving weightlifting exhibitions and sharing my story, explaining why I, the strongest man in the world, needed the strength of Jesus Christ to get through life. About 1974 Jim Adair, then editorial director of Victor Books in Wheaton, Illinois, approached me about writing my autobiography, and I agreed. Because I did not have the time to write my story, Jerry Jenkins, then just beginning his writing career, was assigned to work with me. Since the publication of my autobiography in 1975 Jerry has written some eighty books, including the best-selling *Out of the Blue*, the story of Los Angeles Dodgers pitcher Orel Hershiser.

I am grateful to Jerry, now writer in residence at Moody Bible Institute, Chicago, for his willingness to permit Jim Adair, now retired after forty-three years in publishing, to work with me in producing this updated, expanded edition of *The World's Strongest Man*. Thanks also to my lovely wife, Glenda, my best friend, who has been such a help to me during my weightlifting days and through years of declining health. Glenda's contribution to this book includes an account of how God has seen us through difficult times.

Why does anyone share his story, as I am doing in this autobiography? The truth must be that the individual believes he wants to document various happenings in his life and thinks, justified or not, that his experiences will benefit others. Some simply do it for money or egotistical reasons. My desire is to pay tribute to God, who gave me not only my herculean strength but also much more—spiritual stamina that has carried me through my trials and continues to keep me going today despite spending many of my waking hours directing our Youth Home from a wheelchair.

I feel that those who follow me in life can learn not only from my accomplishments but from my mistakes as well. We should all be students of history! If each generation has to invent the wheel, then little progress will be made in civilization. Therefore, I am passing along many personal experiences, hoping that readers will glean knowledge that will give them a head start on life.

During the past three decades, some people have looked at my traveling schedule and my daily routine at the Paul Anderson Youth Home and admonished, "Paul, you are doing too much. You are burning the candle at both ends." My answer to these dear, caring individuals has been, "But oh, what a beautiful light!"

This sums up my personal philosophy better than I can attempt to explain it. I believe that we, as Christians, should all do as much as we possibly can while our heavenly Father allows us to remain in this life, even if it means pushing. Being an athlete, I certainly think that we need to care for our bodies, the temple of God's Spirit, as Scripture tells us. We should exercise, eat properly, and rest. I admit I haven't rested enough because I have strived to burn the candle far into the night and make as bright a glow as I could.

In listing my records in the pages of this book, I believe I could have achieved greater lifts. It would be fun for me to ask some weightlifting enthusiast if he would like to see pictures of me doing my 450-pound snatch, 600-pound clean and jerk, 1,500-pound squat, 750-pound bench press, and 950-pound dead lift. He would probably respond with an enthusiastic yes. Then I would show him pictures of the Paul Anderson Youth Home, along with photos of some of the thousands of appearances I have made, which I hope had a positive impact on audiences. I honestly feel I could have reached these great plateaus of lifting had I selfishly dwelt on developing my personal strength and not heeded the calling of Almighty God to establish our Youth Home and keep it going through my exhibitions across the country.

While I understand the warm and friendly warnings coming from those who felt I was going to burn out, my answer was and is, "I would rather burn out than rust out."

No one is assured of a tomorrow. Therefore, I continue to do all that I can today. Health problems have slowed me down, yes, but I am still serving my Lord as Glenda and I operate the Paul Anderson Youth Home.

Paul Anderson's Lifting Accomplishments

World Champion
Olympic Champion
9 World Records
18 American Records
Twice USA National Champion
Retired unbeaten as an amateur
First man to total 1,100 pounds in three Olympic lifts
First man to snatch 300 pounds squat style
First man to press 400 pounds
First man to lift 450 pounds from floor to overhead
First man to lift from the shoulders 500 pounds overhead
First man to lift from the shoulders 600 pounds overhead

Box appearing with article "The Uplifting Story of
Paul Anderson" by Bob Barnett and Bob Carroll
in the *Saturday Evening Post,* p. 59, November 1988

A
Greater
Strength

1

No Apologies

It didn't just happen. I worked long and hard at it. Then, in the early 1950s, the title was mine: the World's Strongest Man. I ceased to claim this title after I stopped doing public exhibitions and defending such an identity. I believe I can claim the more prestigious position of being "history's strongest human." By all records, I do have a right to this title. When I was in my prime years, I believe I was stronger and potentially stronger than anyone who ever performed in the strength realm.

Even after I retired from performing, it bugged me when people would ask me if I was still lifting weights. Of course I was still lifting. Would I have looked the way I did if I weren't?

I wasn't huge because I was a big eater. It was the daily lifting and stimulating of my muscles that added bulk, along with consuming the proper foods. That is also what kept me in good physical condition, and I enjoyed it.

People outside the weightlifting world find it difficult to believe I continued to train and stay in condition even past the age of forty. They assumed that all men are finished athletically when they pass their fortieth birthday. This is certainly not correct. In reality, a man can maintain his strength far into his senior years if he trains regularly, eats properly, and is not plagued with some type of illness, as I have been in recent years.

Later, we will discuss the physical aspects of my accomplishments more. For now I'll tell you that I'm basically a "bad" person. That's right. My basic personality is not good, but I'm not as mean and rough as my gruff voice sounds. I've always been a loner, and I never liked my privacy invaded. I'm still hard to get along with, and I'm constantly battling with myself, trying to be a nicer guy.

Why admit that? Simple. It proves that being a Christian, being a child of God, is a gift. If Christianity were a contest, I'd finish last. I couldn't earn the love of God. The Bible teaches that man falls short of God's glory, and here again, I am living proof.

But God chose to love me, and I chose to accept that love and receive Him into my heart, so now He and I are working on making me a better person. I'm always getting in the way, but God is using me in spite of myself. Long ago, He took my concern for young people, my physical strength, and my ability to speak in public and used these gifts for His glory.

I enjoyed the years I was on the road. I couldn't get enough of it. When one challenge was over, I moved on to the next. I didn't sleep much, and it seemed I was always on the go. Challenges are the fabric of life, and I am going to continue doing what the Lord has called me to do: provide a Christian home for misguided young men and spread His message.

I'm not sure just when it was that I became so obsessed with success and challenges, but maybe my story will give you a clue.

I was born October 17, 1932, in Toccoa, Georgia, the son of a construction man; his father was a pastor of the Christian Church in Temple, Georgia. My parents, my sister, Dot, and I moved around a lot because Daddy worked on various projects, including the Tennessee Valley Authority. My father, Bob, was a friendly, hardworking man who seldom said much about his beliefs. He just liked to see things built and have a hand in their building.

My mother, Ethel, was the up-front Christian. We grew up close to her relatives, primarily solid Baptists, Methodists, and Christian Church members. My commitment to Christ wouldn't come until the 1956 Olympic Games, but I received a great deal of exposure to Christianity during those formative years.

I was twenty-one months old when we first moved. Daddy had found work during the Great Depression of the early thirties at a Civilian Conservation Corps (CCC) camp near Franklin, North Carolina, and we moved there. The CCC camps were set up by Franklin D. Roosevelt's New Deal program in 1933 to give employment to young men for public conservation projects. My first memory is of seeing our dog, Prince, through the screen door and knowing we were at a new place.

I even remember my first real spanking. I am sure I had received some punishment whacks before this occasion, but I was severely punished this time. It was after we had moved to Franklin and were living with an elderly man, Mr. Stiles, who had a tiny mimosa tree planted and protected in the yard. It was a prized possession. We were supposedly too far north for a mimosa tree to survive, so he had it surrounded with stakes. I wasn't yet four years old, but already I was seeking challenges. The most exciting challenge I could think of was coming as close to that tree as I could in my wagon without hitting it.

I came tooling down a hillside and went careening into the yard, smashing that finger-sized tree. "My mimosa! My mimosa!" Mr. Stiles cried.

Later, I cried too.

When I was nearly six, we relocated with Daddy to a Tennessee Valley Authority (TVA) project near Murphy, North Carolina. I started school at Reeds Chapel Elementary and Junior High School. The first three grades were taught in the same classroom, and with all those children of different ages, strict discipline was necessary. I was always getting caressed with the big paddle, usually because of Elmer Blair. No matter what Elmer did, I cracked up. Even when he was not trying to be funny, he was hilarious. The more serious the situation in our primitive schoolroom, the funnier Elmer would become. There was no getting away from him because we both sat in the same desk, which was customary for the little ones in that day.

I was the youngest and, as strange as it may seem now, the smallest kid in the classroom. Anna Lou Keenum was our teacher, and I did what I had to do to get her attention. Mostly, I was a tattletale. If I heard someone say that someone else had said a cussword, I'd quickly pass along the secondhand information to Miss Keenum, and the alleged cusser would get whipped. I was just the kind of youngster I can hardly tolerate today!

I would much rather have been big and tough, but in the meantime, I settled for being fast and a tattler. Just when I had learned how to run and play as well as almost anyone, and just when I started to keep track of whom I could or could not whip, I was stricken with Bright's disease, a chronic inflammation of the kidneys that generally leads to end-stage kidney failure later in life. I wasn't even six years of age yet, and I was sick and not getting better. This was before the days of antibiotics, and it wasn't long before I was dying in the hospital in Murphy.

My grandfather on my mother's side called in a pastor friend who directed an orphanage. He and my family prayed through the night, and I still believe that it was only God's answer to their prayers that kept me alive.

Back at school weeks later, I was restricted from too much activity. It almost killed me. Glancing around the room at the blackboard (which was just that, a wall that had been painted black) and the potbellied stove, I ached to be outside. I wasn't popular in school anyway because I was new and sickly. I wore knickers while everyone else wore overalls, and I felt the peer pressure.

Finally, I disobeyed. Running, jumping, and fighting, I reestablished my place in the world, and life again was worth living. My mother disobeyed the doctor's orders too. She had been feeding me broth and other light dishes but hadn't been seeing any improvement. Finally, she started filling me with protein foods, and I responded immediately. In later years, the memory of how her new diet affected me helped me devise a revolutionary high-protein diet for weightlifters.

For as long as I live, I'll never forget all that went with living in the Murphy mountains. Mountain funerals were something else. I remember one funeral that began at three o'clock in the afternoon and ended at five when the undertaker interrupted with, ''We've got to get this man buried before it gets too dark!'' The dead man's friends had gone through every custom they could think of for the funeral. They rang the church bell sixty times for the years he had lived, and they requested that those who would join the dear brother in heaven to file past and shake hands with the pastor. They even asked for anyone at all who had anything to say about the deceased to come up and share it.

One of my funniest memories is of an evangelistic service in the small church we attended. I suppose if I'd been paying more attention to the fiery preacher I might have made a decision for Christ at an earlier age, but on this particular night, there was a distraction.

A mentally handicapped woman always came to church with her mother, who had to treat her like a child. The daughter had a tobacco-chewing habit, but her mother forbade her to chew in church. Midway through the service, the mother noticed that the daughter was chomping on a real mouthful. With little tact, she insisted that her daughter throw it out the window.

The daughter made quite a project of removing the chaw from her jaw and attempting to throw the ugly brown mass out a window over the heads of several ducking people. Unfortunately, the window was closed! Her aim was a little off anyway; the clod splattered at the top of the pane and began to slowly slide down, oozing to the bottom of the sill during the next few minutes. Every eye in the place was on the mess on the window. I was only six at the time, but I'll never forget it.

Another clear memory is of a prayer meeting held at our house. I had been playing outside for a few hours when it got dark, and I decided it was time to go in. I was running for home as fast as I could (I always pretended I could run one hundred miles an hour). As I got near the house, I stubbed my toe on a root sticking up through the sidewalk, and the pain went all the way to my head.

I kept running, half limping, staggering into the house, where I figured I would be due some real sympathy and attention. As I entered the house, I noticed the prayer meeting in progress. My mother stopped my howling with a "you'd better not make a sound" look. There I sat in excruciating pain, unable to relieve myself with a holler for more than fifteen minutes during prayer meeting!

We moved back to Toccoa in 1941, on to a little town in Tennessee in 1942, and again to Toccoa in time for me to begin fourth grade that fall. Finally we were in one place to stay for a while. Daddy still moved around a lot, but he usually came home on weekends. He wasn't the disciplinarian that I am today, but he was a giving type of man and a good father. There were times when he should have been home and wasn't, I guess, but the same can be said about most fathers (me, for sure, during my traveling days).

My best friend in junior and senior high school was Harold Tanner. He and I were interested in the same sports. We were highly competitive and fought as much as we played, but it was fun. I remember many times I promised Harold that, if he came by and woke me up at 5:00 A.M., I would go hunting with him. Then at 5:00 A.M. I'd suddenly change my mind. Hunting squirrels and deer couldn't compete with a cozy bed at that time of day.

There was no twelfth grade at Toccoa High. It was a city school with almost four hundred students in grades eight through eleven. You could graduate at sixteen and go on to college.

I had gained size and strength in athletics and became part of the "in crowd." Because I was one of only three guys in the school who owned a car, played blocking back in a single-wing offense on the football team, and was a class officer and active in the lettermen's club, I had all the dates I wanted. I seldom cracked a book because back then it was bad to be either a scholar or a drunk. We were just straight, clean, nonstudying athletes, and we thought we were cool.

My parents weren't as strict as they might have been, but I was a pretty good kid. I never got into serious trouble and was able to come and go as I pleased. I worked in a filling station pumping gas and drying cars after another fellow had washed them. On Saturday afternoons I'd worry that I might not get finished in time for dates, and often in the winter the water would freeze on the cars. However, I always worked hard and long and felt better when I had something to do.

My parents moved to another construction job just before my last year in high school, so I stayed in Toccoa with my sister, Dot, and her husband, Julius. I still didn't study much and goofed around a lot, but being a varsity football player kept me out of trouble.

It bothered me that many of the colleges offering me scholarships were also offering scholarships to dozens of other guys. It was flattering to have someone offer to pay my way to school, but I didn't want to be just another one of eighty freshmen football players. The majority of the schools that contacted me were running a T formation, which meant they saw me as a possible pulling guard, but I didn't want to play on the line. I liked the backfield.

Anyway, it seemed that the big universities were signing many athletes in order to be sure that their opponents didn't recruit them. There was little chance that all of them would play, but they wined them, dined them, and signed them. I was treated to weekends at some of the big schools and was even offered a couple of suits of clothes.

I visited several big schools, but I was most intrigued by a little Baptist college, Furman (now a university), in Greenville, South Carolina. The school was offering only eleven scholarships and ran an offense I felt would best utilize my bulk and surprising speed in the backfield.

I decided to go, but I wasn't prepared for how lonely, out of place, and frustrated I would be. Neither was I prepared for my chance introduction to weightlifting, a meeting that would change my life. Weightlifting was officially looked down on by both high school and college coaches. It had a bad reputation from comic book ads and muscle magazines. Some thought it would hamper flexibility and make an athlete muscle-bound. It was forbidden to athletes, especially those on scholarships. However, at Furman I would discover lifting in secret.

2

Weightlifting Fever

Had I gone to a big university, I probably wouldn't have been able to play varsity ball until I was at least a junior. Big schools simply had too many players. However, at Furman, because they gave only eleven scholarships in 1950, I played in all the freshman games and looked forward to playing varsity as a sophomore.

Football was about all I enjoyed. Everyone else but me seemed to have a goal. They were working toward degrees in business administration or physical education. I didn't see much future in either area, so I didn't know what my future held. I was like a fish out of water and became depressed.

I had not learned any good study habits, and at Furman I was in a tough school, forced to study to keep my grades high enough for football. In the past, my life had been pretty well regulated for me by high school schedules; now I was on my own, supposedly making decisions about my future. I didn't care about anything.

After the football season was over in 1950, I was invited to go with a couple of classmates to pick up a set of weights they had left at a summer camp. Bob Snead, a classmate from West Virginia who owned the weights, set them up in a room above the gymnasium just off the indoor balcony track at Furman. Bob and his buddies didn't publicize their regular workouts, fearing the coaches would find out. I visited Bob and the other guys once in a while, just to tease them or goof around with the weights.

Bob Snead was a dedicated weightlifter, a real muscle man. He worked hard and didn't appreciate my making fun of him or playfully pulling a heavy bar full of weights off the rack. Being somewhat a perfectionist, I didn't want to get seriously involved unless I was going to go whole hog. Since I didn't see much to it, I felt inclined to discourage Bob and his weightlifting friends with my wisecracks.

Often I would take all the weights off a bar, then flip the bar around and do unusual maneuvers with it. Once I did a one-hand snatch (bringing the bar from the floor up over my head in one move) with the same amount of weight Bob was using for a more difficult strength-building exercise. My show-off trick was simply a display of strength. Bob wasn't into that. It didn't make sense to him to show off. He said lifting would help an athlete to be better in whatever sport he was involved. The weights were simply for bodybuilding.

Anyway, I thought it would be pretty impressive to lift with one hand a bar with weights that he had struggled with on another exercise, but I didn't have my hand correctly centered and the weights shifted. With no collars on either end of the bar, the plates slid off one end; of course the bar shifted, sending plates at the other end crashing to the floor. One twenty-five-pound plate rolled out the door and almost dropped to the gym below before Bob snatched it. Had it fallen, it might have killed the basketball coach directing a practice session, not to mention putting a fatal dent in the secret weightlifting program!

In time I decided to take Bob's weightlifting a bit more seriously. He and his friends were doing quarter knee bends with perhaps four hundred pounds of weights on their shoulders. It looked like something I could handle, so I took the bar. The other guys were amazed when I did a deep knee bend. This gave me great satisfaction and increased my interest in the sport. If just lifting a few hundred pounds of weights could gain me recognition, then maybe I had found something!

My venture into lifting, however, was the only activity that satisfied me. School was becoming more and more a drag. I didn't seem to care about doing anything—certainly not studying. The Korean War was hot, and lots of guys were leaving school to enlist. I decided I wanted to leave too. Not to enlist. Not for anything special. I simply wanted to leave.

My parents had moved to Elizabethton, Tennessee, so I moved in with them. They were disappointed that I had left Furman before the end of my first year; however, I assured them that I planned to go back, though I didn't know why. There was little there for me, unless it was the hope of becoming a coach, which didn't interest me, or eventually playing pro football after a successful college career. However, that didn't excite me either, for in those days NFL salaries were peanuts compared with what they are today. Obviously, I was without definite goals, and my parents were worried. For almost a year I did nothing but rebuild a 1934 Ford and drive my mother back and forth to see her relatives in Toccoa. I simply wanted to clear my mind and regroup. I enjoyed weightlifting and lifted some during the year, but it wasn't until the spring of 1952 that I really got into it seriously.

My brother-in-law, Julius, had given me some weights and I worked out with them, but suddenly I wanted a greater challenge. I determined to see what I could really do in the deep knee bend. I visited junkyards and bought automobile axles and drive shafts for bars, two-by-fours for racks, and buckets and barrels in which to form concrete weights. When I assembled my bar, I attached the concrete weights with chains, which made it an ominous-looking piece of equipment. As close as I could figure, I had assembled approximately five hundred pounds of weights on one bar.

For more than six months, I did the only exercise I knew: the deep knee bend. With the bar a few inches lower than my shoulders, I put my head under it so it would rest behind my neck; with the bar extending at an equal length on each side straight across my upper back and shoulders, I moved away from the racks and went down into a full knee bend, rose, walked forward, and placed the weight back on the racks. I repeated this exercise many times in my workouts.

My social life had been a zero since moving back home because I was neither collegian nor high schooler; I kept pretty much to myself and enjoyed it that way. I ran into some fellows who lifted and who followed the weightlifting magazines. The local fellows talked lifting with me; they were really shocked when they saw my weights. I had built my body weight up to 275 pounds and was lifting a bar that might have killed another lifter. No one wanted to try it, but neither did they believe that I really had 500 pounds on it. From reading the muscle books, I knew I was capable of the deep knee bend record.

My friends always talked about Bob Peoples, who lived not far away in the north Georgia hills. He held the world record in the dead lift at 725 pounds and was a legend in those parts, though he was forty-two years old and no longer active in competition. (The dead lift involves lifting the bar off the floor as you rise to a standing position. Since you're lifting the weight only a couple of feet off the floor and not doing anything with it once it is lifted, the record in the dead lift has always been higher than in any of the other power lifts.)

I'll never forget the day my weightlifting friends took me to meet Bob Peoples. He lived in an old farmhouse on a hill in limestone country and did his weightlifting in a dungeonlike dugout cellar with a dirt floor. It was dark, dank, and depressing, but he had good equipment. His racks were lodged in the wall and were made of big railroad ties.

I was a little surprised at Peoples' physique. His arms were unusually long and his hands were huge. I was certain it was the killer dead lift that had stretched him out of shape, until I met his father, a nonlifter from whom Bob had obviously inherited his physique. Bob's build had contributed to his dead lift, not vice versa.

"Would you like to lift a little?" Peoples asked me in his shy, nonassertive way.

"Sure," I said. "I'll try a deep knee bend or two."

"What weight would you like to warm up with?" he asked. I had never heard of warming up, for my practice had been to assemble all the weights I could and "give 'er a try."

"What?" I asked.

"What would you like to warm up with?" At the time, I had been reading that the world record in the deep knee bend had been 575 pounds. I figured if I could do 500 pounds a number of times, I ought to be able to do 600 pounds at least once, the world record notwithstanding.

"Six hundred pounds," I said. My three friends laughed. A smile escaped Bob Peoples. He loaded the bar with six hundred pounds but cautioned the others to stay close and spot me. With the bar across my shoulders, I dropped to a full squat and rose steadily, never wavering. When I was erect for a second, I squatted fully again and stood. They could hardly believe it. I had done the deep knee bend *twice* with a weight that had never before been used *once* in the same lift. Peoples and other local muscle men were speechless.

With their reaction, I was hooked. It was a thrill to show what I could do. I had never lifted in competition, but I knew I was capable. Back home I read all the record books and the technique manuals and tried all the new lifts I had learned. My lifting decreased in poundage during the two or three weeks following my meeting with Bob Peoples, however. I had become so psyched up from the visit that I overworked.

Rather than building my strength, I was tearing it down. One of my assets, I was to learn in later years, was that I possessed a tremendous rate of metabolism. My muscle tissue repaired and rebuilt more rapidly than the average man's. Weightlifting is the ultimate exercise, but I was working harder and faster than even my accelerated metabolism. I soon realized the problem and became a smarter lifter.

I worked out often with Bob Peoples, but my lifts were about 20 percent below normal when I was in his depressing dungeon. That just wasn't a good environment for positive thinking, a key in lifting and life. Bob taught me not only how to warm up properly but also how to do several "assistance" lifts, which built strength and stamina for the contest lifts.

I couldn't seem to get enough of the action. I entered some local contests, but no one was in my weight class, and my deep knee bends were done only for exhibitions. I still enjoyed lifting, though I looked forward to some bona fide competition. It would have surprised me to find anyone anywhere who could outlift me.

By the fall of 1952, I had decided not to go back to college in order to concentrate on lifting. I was getting lots of encouragement from Bob Peoples and the other local enthusiasts; lifting was doing wonders for my ego. I was just one of many weightlifters in the United States, but it was becoming increasingly obvious, at least to me and other area lifters, that I was one of the best.

However, I was only known locally. I wasn't getting the publicity I deserved because I was not lifting competitively. I was not lifting in the big meets because I wasn't known well enough to be invited. It was a stalemate. All I could do was keep lifting long and hard and heavy and be ready, when my chance came, to show the experts what I could do.

My first meet was in Chattanooga, at which I broke all Tennessee state records, but I was met with apprehension from the old-time lifters because of my size.

In 1953, I performed in a meet in Atlanta and was equally successful there. The only other meet I attended was the North American championships in Montreal, where I won over Norbert Schemansky, then the world record holder in two of the three Olympic lifts. Unfortunately, my injuries and illnesses generally kept me out of other meets; there was a feeling that I was simply dodging open competition and that some of the lifts I reported were only fantasies.

I perfected my technique in the three Olympic lifts of that day: the press, the snatch, and the clean and jerk. At the same time, I wisely began studying nutrition. I developed combinations of food supplements and high-protein diets that would add bulk and strength to my body as I lifted. Word of my strength gradually began to circulate, and I started competing more frequently. I never lost, dominating every lift in every meet I entered.

During the late spring of 1953, I began looking toward the tryouts for the United States Amateur Athletic Union team, which was to compete in the world championships in Stockholm that year. Though I had been discovered by the weightlifting magazines, that didn't necessarily help me get an invitation to the AAU tryouts, because my lifts were so far superior to lifts by other amateurs that the magazine stories were considered exaggerations. The AAU wasn't going to take me seriously until the experts saw me with their own eyes.

I was beginning to realize that I could probably lift more than anyone in the world, and that excited me. With each day, my lifting became more important to me. I tried anything and everything that would make me stronger, but I never tried to shortcut hard work. It seemed that everything I did pointed toward the world championships. I daydreamed often about how surprised the coaches and other team members would be when they discovered at the tryouts that the strongest lifter in the world was an unknown from the hills of north Georgia.

One of the training techniques I employed to strengthen my back, legs, and torso was to hook a heavy object to a leather belt around my waist and heft it off the ground by standing up. I knew at 5'9" I would have to develop my pulling power because that was supposedly the weakness of a short-of-stature lifter. I got to the point where I could lift tremendous poundage.

While living for a time in east Tennessee, where my father was working on a hydroelectric plant, I began looking for something to really test me. My body weight was increasing along with my strength, bulk, and enthusiasm. I built a platform in the yard that allowed me to set a heavy object on the ground five feet beneath it. I would stand on the platform and squat to hook the belt to the object, then rise until I was standing upright and lifting the object off the ground.

I finally found something I knew would test me and add to my strength if I could master it. It was an old manganese safe with extremely thick walls, and it was tremendously heavy. I had escalated its poundage by filling it with weights and concrete. After I welded it shut and added slots for the belt connections, I found myself with thirty-five hundred pounds to struggle against.

To my knowledge, no one had ever before attempted such a lift.

For a while, I couldn't budge the weight. I would hitch myself into position and pull slowly against the force, building strength in my legs in what today is known as isometric fashion. Finally, the day came when I budged that monstrous safe. What a feeling to know I was moving more weight than anyone else had ever even attempted! Few believed I could do it, or that the old safe weighed as much as I claimed, but future feats would convince them. Meanwhile, I was regularly doing lifts with the safe, spending hours alone on that five-foot wood platform, building my leg, back, and torso muscles into bulging sinews.

To maintain my flexibility and agility, I ran quite a bit; once I was timed eleven seconds flat for the one-hundred-yard dash. I could do a split, touch my toes, and jump from a flat-footed squat to the top of a three-foot table with little effort.

About a month before the tryouts for the world championships in Stockholm, I spent an afternoon working with the old safe. I lifted it several times, perhaps more than I had ever done in one day. This was making me far and away the best lifter anywhere, and I looked forward to the grueling workouts. I even looked forward to the beef extract (the liquids of beef with a little salt); it tasted horrible but was a necessary ingredient in rebuilding my muscles and supplementing my diet.

Later that evening, after having rested for a few hours, I felt like lifting the old safe with its assortment of junk weights a couple more times before bed. It wouldn't do much for my strength, but I was beginning to enjoy it and figured it would be good for my confidence.

Without warming up, which, unfortunately, was still not my practice, I hitched up the belt and began a slow pull against the weight. The safe wouldn't budge! I thought perhaps the cool night air or the few hours of relaxation might have taken off my edge. I carefully strained against it again. Still nothing! I began breathing deeply in the blackness of the evening. I tensed my muscles from shoulders to ankles. I heaved, grunted, pulled, and strained. My veins bulged. My head ached. I drove my feet hard into the platform and wiggled slowly from side to side as if trying to escape the restraining belt. This weight would not defeat me. It could not. I was cold, perhaps, but I would work myself to the point of lifting it again this day, if only one more time.

I began to hate the weight. It had taken on a personality. It was defying me. It had made me work and sweat all afternoon, and I had conquered it. Now it was taking its revenge. Strangely, it seemed to have gained weight and strength on its own since I had last lifted it. (This feeling toward weights began to dominate my psyche in competition. While other lifters would take several minutes to stare at the weight and get themselves all worked up over the lift, I simply would stride to the bar and lift it. I hated it. It caused me pain and work; I wanted to quickly take the victory.)

I had worked my body into a flame of strength battling against the weight of the safe, and now I was ready for the final pull. I never doubted that I could lift the weight. I never allowed that type of thought to enter my mind. Once I conquered a weight, it was mine forever. There were times when my maximum lifting strength was down a couple of percentage points, but anytime a weight defeated me it was because of physical reasons, not mental ones. Until I triumphed over the weight and it crashed to the floor, I was always convinced that I could lift it.

Now I was convinced I could lift the safe. Everything else had been preliminary. What had begun as an ego satisfier, one last lift before bed, had turned into a gross challenge of my strength. I held my breath, lifted my head, closed my eyes, and clenched my teeth. My body (now nearly three hundred pounds of muscle) shook as I exploded against the thirty-five-hundred-pound safe. My fingers dug into my palms, and finally I stood erect, but the safe had not yielded. The leather strap had stretched about six inches, and the muscles in my right leg had also stretched. I had seriously injured myself, and I couldn't understand how the weight I had mastered earlier could have defeated me.

I hobbled into the house and applied hot packs to my knee, not knowing, as we do today, that I should have used ice. When the hot packs were in place, a great deal of blood and water were drawn into the knee and caused more damage. I stayed up all night, thinking that if I went to sleep, I would be unable to straighten my leg.

During ensuing days, I held on to a faint hope for the AAU tryouts, although it was in vain. The incredible strength I had built up for over a year had ironically been directed against my leg. I had come near ruining my body with my own strength.

I discovered later that, between the time I had last lifted the safe and the time it stubbornly refused to budge, dew had set in and the night air had frozen the safe to the ground! The only way I could have lifted that safe was to have lifted the whole side of that Tennessee hill with it!

Weightlifting had by now become my entire life. I had refrained from smoking, drinking, and worldly vices in the past because of my reputation and my Christian training; now I lived clean because I had a goal. I wanted to be known as the strongest man in the world. It was frustrating to know that, though I was lifting more than anyone else, most experts were still unaware of me. I knew I needed only one chance to show them, but the thirty-five-hundred-pound safe, frozen to the ground, had kept me from the AAU tryouts and the world championships.

In spite of this, I knew my day would come.

3
Frustration

In high school and college, I had enjoyed a somewhat active social life. As a serious weightlifter, I became withdrawn, a social dropout. I had one quest, and I would not be stopped. Nothing else mattered.

As soon as my injured leg was strong enough to support a little weight, I furiously exercised it, increasing the poundage it could endure. There were many long hours and grueling days involved in rebuilding, but the work paid off. As is so often the case, the injured part of my anatomy became the strongest, stronger even than in its original state. My legs became the key in my accelerated drive to be not just the best weightlifter but so far out of reach that there would be no competition. I was capable of achieving the goal, although it would take everything I had to give. I was still virtually unheard of, though the weights with which I practiced were much heavier than those lifted for the existing world records.

In fact, one evening as I practiced in an old gym, I broke three existing world records. Ironically, it was the same day a new world champion was crowned in the big meet in Stockholm. Each of my three lifts was better than the lifts of the champ, and I outdid his total by about fifty pounds.

In those days, I was doing knee bends with 800 pounds, bench pressing at nearly 500, and dead lifting over 700—all accomplishments dwarfing or equaling recognized world records. In the official Olympic lifts, I was pressing almost 400 pounds when the Olympic record was 330; I was snatching 335 when the record was 325; I was clean and jerking 426 when the record was 415. I realize this is difficult to believe, but I had "cried wolf" so many times, I could not get on the team that went to some of these championships.

One thing was certain: I had no mental blocks about any weight. Perhaps if I had been cognizant of the world records before I started lifting, I would have set some barriers in my mind. By the time I was aware of the records, I was already breaking them. However, none of my records would be recognized until they were set in competition. Until then, I was afraid even to mention them, because no one would have believed me.

I began winning state contests, and by the spring of 1954 I was looking forward to the AAU national championships, planned for June in Indianapolis. Though in practice I was breaking national and world records, I had been playing it conservatively in state contests, lifting only enough to win and maybe set a state record. I was saving my real show for a YMCA meet scheduled for Philadelphia not long before the Indianapolis nationals. I wanted to hit Indianapolis with a world record under my belt from the Philly meet. Then making the AAU team for the World Games would be my next quest!

I didn't want to go unnoticed in the Philadelphia event. This was the time to establish myself. For my first lift, the press, I asked for more than the world record to be put on the bar. I didn't need to prove that I could come near the record. I already knew that. I didn't want to work up to it. I wanted to break it on the first lift and reset it in the same meet. The officials and the crowds were dubious about my brash move; here was an unknown with a couple of Southern state records who thought he was going to break a world record—and without even working up to it. Sure!

I wasn't worried. They loaded the bar; I bent to grasp it cleanly. In the press, the lifter brings the bar to his chest, then pushes it above his head without moving his legs or any other part of his body. It is a more difficult lift than the clean and jerk, because the jerk involves simply pressing the weight over your head; you are allowed to bend your knees and jerk your body to add momentum. (Because there were so many ways to put the weight overhead, the International Weightlifting Federation has eliminated the press from competition.)

My adrenaline was flowing; I was anxious to quickly bring the bar to my chest, get a good feel of it, and then drive it over my head. The world record at that time was about 330 pounds, and I had asked for 350 for my first attempt. Everyone was skeptical, but I felt it was just a matter of lifting and winning.

As I rose with the bar, I knew this was going to be an easy lift. I had practiced with much more weight, and the bar actually felt lighter than I expected. When I brought it to my chest and flipped my wrists to get them under the bar for the press, my foot slipped and the bar snapped my left wrist clean. No one could believe anything except that the incredible weight had broken my wrist. Philadelphian lifting enthusiasts were sympathetic, but it was clear to them that I had needlessly injured myself by foolishly attempting a weight that no one in the world was yet capable of pressing.

My wrist was put in a cast by an orthopedic surgeon, but as soon as I got back home to Elizabethton I went to work on the cast. I didn't like the looks of other arms I had seen come out of casts. The Indianapolis national championships were out of the question for me, and I needed something to occupy my mind until

I could work out at full strength again. I never once considered giving up the sport, not when I was breaking world records regularly behind closed doors. The sport needed me; I wanted the world to know about my capabilities in breaking weightlifting records, especially after my leg and arm injuries had made me appear somewhat foolish.

I did a lot of leg work but found lifting with one hand no help at all. I needed to exercise my upper arm muscles, even if I had to somehow bypass the broken bone. I was familiar enough with the anatomy to know exercising an injured arm would speed recovery. Though I don't recommend the following without medical supervision, I did this on my own: I cut off the cast just above the break and rebuilt it shorter and closer to the wrist. Then I molded a brace for my upper arm out of tin and took the model to a machine shop and had a brace made from steel with a rod protruding from it. When the apparatus was finished, I attached it to my arm above the cast and rigged the rod so that it could either pull or push weights. I lifted nearly as much poundage with my "fake" arm as I did when I was healthy. While I was bypassing the break and putting the pressure on my upper arm, lifting caused blood to circulate through the entire arm. The broken wrist healed quickly. Some might have thought my procedure dangerous and foolish, but no doctor could deny that it resulted in faster healing and an arm that was as strong as ever.

As the arm healed, I looked forward to the 1954 World Games to be held in Vienna. I was determined that there would be no stopping me this time. My body weight had increased to 310 pounds, then surged to 325 when my arm was back to normal and my lifting activity increased. We moved back to Toccoa, where I began an intense series of workouts, which led to the AAU trials. I wanted so badly to be on the United States AAU team for the Vienna world championships I could taste it.

My totals in workouts were increasing at an incredible rate, and I was lifting one hundred more total pounds in the three lifts than the world records of that day. Again, I knew it was just a matter of going to the meet, lifting, and winning. I was beginning to long more than ever for the opportunity to break the world records. I kept most of my accomplishments to myself and continually checked my totals and the accuracy of my scales and weights. I was certain that after the Vienna championships, the world would know.

For months I had become obsessed with workouts and the upcoming trials for the AAU team. I was careful not to exhaust myself and had developed an effective training program. It was intense and punishing, yet I had a sense of pace and direction. I found myself spent but eager to return for more each day. My metabolism was racing, and my body was becoming a weight-lifting machine. It was exhilarating.

When some buddies came by about two weeks before the trials and asked if I wanted to join them to see the stock car races, I felt I deserved a night out. Hours of lifting that day had left me drained. I needed the break.

W.O. Couch, a friend from high school, was driving, and he had a car full of guys. It had been a hot day, so the light rain that began as we pulled away from my house was refreshing. Couch wasn't speeding or driving recklessly, but when he passed a car and pulled back into the right lane, his car began hydroplaning and suddenly we were spinning. I remember hoping I wouldn't get broken up too badly.

As we left the road and plowed through a barbed-wire fence, I thought only of survival. Tryouts and championships or not, I just wanted to come out of this in one piece. We finally slammed into a tree on my side of the car. Though the others suffered only a few scratches, I had several broken ribs, and I was sure my hip had been injured too.

At a little South Carolina hospital, doctors confirmed the broken ribs, although they didn't have an X-ray machine strong enough to shoot through my hip. I was sent to Atlanta, where the hip injury was also confirmed, a misfortune that would cause me problems years later.

During the next weeks, I was discouraged but not bitter. There was little I could do except get back in shape and keep studying nutrition and anatomy. I developed new training techniques and continued to increase my lifting poundage. I knew that if the day ever came when I could enter a prestigious meet healthy, I would really put on a show.

During 1954 I entered more local, state, and regional contests and broke several records. Offers began pouring in. Money-hungry agents wanted me to become a professional strong man. It was intriguing, and the money sounded good, but I wanted those amateur world records. The pro records had always been clouded by a lack of regulation or a governing body. Odds were that all the pro records were exaggerated or rigged anyway, and the whole seamy life didn't appeal to me. Strangely, later it would. Unfortunately, I would get caught up in it, but for now, I still hoped for a chance to demonstrate my ability in amateur competition.

Then I heard the news: In addition to the scheduled World Championships to be held in Munich, Germany, in October, the United States weightlifting team had an additional international trip planned for 1955. Our team would meet the Russians in the Soviet Union sometime during the month of June. American athletes would actually go behind the Iron Curtain. I determined to get healthy, stay healthy, and make that team. No Americans, much less athletes, had been behind the Iron Curtain for so long that the entire country was excited about it. I couldn't think of anything I would rather do. I worked hard, hoping against hope that there would be no more bad breaks to keep me out of the competition. I knew I wouldn't be eliminated by any better lifters, because there were none. However, I had no idea that I might not even have a chance to try out for the team.

4

"A Wonder of Nature"

With my heart set on going to Russia, I had to make my pitch to Bob Hoffman, coach of the United States AAU weightlifting team. He was a promoter and owner of the York Barbell Company, York, Pennsylvania.

I got the runaround and wound up talking with several other people at York, but when I finally got hold of Hoffman, he gave me the bad word. Norbert Schemansky of Detroit, the world champion, wanted to go. Hoffman figured Schemansky was entitled to it after setting records and representing the team so well in international competition.

"I can lift far more than he can," I reasoned.

"Well, I've heard that," Hoffman said, "but we've never seen you produce." The team wasn't impressed with the small-time meets in which I had competed. Records from those meets have a way of becoming exaggerated, so no one put much stock in a record unless it was in a meet sanctioned by the AAU.

For all Hoffman knew, I was what some would call a gym athlete: one who can perform in practice but can't cut it before a crowd. Even if my records in small-time weightlifting meets were accurate, who could say what I'd do with the world watching?

"We'll be leaving the day after the National Championships," Hoffman said.

"What if I do well in the championships and beat Schemansky?"

"That'll be up to him. We want to use the same team we used in the Pan American Games in Mexico City last month. If he wants to go, he goes."

I was just twenty-one years old and anxious to prove to the world that I could break existing records. I had been stopped short by three freak injuries, and now that I was finally healthy, it seemed there was little chance I would get my opportunity.

I've always had a positive mental attitude, even during recovery periods after injuries. I decided not to give up but rather work hard and earn my way on to the AAU team for that Russian trip. The national finals in Cleveland were coming up, and I would need inoculations and a passport if I wanted to leave for Russia the day after the competition.

Back then there was about a two-week delay in getting passport papers, but through contacts in Atlanta and at Fort McPherson and a personal trip to Washington, D.C., I got my passport in a matter of days and was ready for the trip. It was then that I learned about the plan of my friends.

They wanted to put pressure on Hoffman and his York Barbell Company and the AAU by sending telegrams from all over the country, urging that I be given a place on the team going to Russia. They would have various trucker friends send telegrams from different cities throughout the United States, making it appear that I had nationwide support. I chuckled about the idea but didn't take part in the scheme. I wouldn't have allowed them to do it if I hadn't deserved the opportunity to make the Russian trip. I had been overlooked when a team was chosen (without tryouts) for the Pan American Games in Mexico City, and it seemed there was no way to break the chain. I would have felt guilty about the telegrams if I hadn't thought I could come through and prove my worth. How much good the telegrams did is hard to say. Hoffman probably just shrugged them off.

When I got to the national finals, I discovered that Schemansky was unable to compete; a chronic back injury had flared up. This also meant he would not go to Russia, but I realized I was not an automatic replacement. Hoffman didn't know if I had a passport and shots or even whether I could lift well enough to qualify. If no one in the meet lifted impressively enough to merit a spot on the team, the team would simply go without a heavyweight. It had been done before.

Yet I was excited. I knew that while world records were usually broken by just a few pounds at a time, I would knock their eyes out with large margins in each lift.

I was ready. I had developed an intensive training program with the most intricate series of exercises and lifts conceivable. My diet consisted primarily of liquid protein, and I drank gallons of milk each day. I had figured a way to consume the correct foods so that my body would become a metabolism machine that burned protein and rebuilt muscle tissue almost as fast as I could tear it down. For some reason, my body broke down protein foods better and more quickly than anyone else I've ever known. Every day my muscles grew and my body weight steadily increased. I could lift more with every passing day, and finally I was at the nationals in Cleveland with something to show. I weighed a few pounds over 340 and didn't even have an official United States uniform, and there was no time for one to be made for me.

When my turn came, I quickly asked for what I considered the maximum weight I could handle with ease in each lift and used just one effort in each event. I broke Schemansky's world record of 425 pounds in the clean and jerk with a lift of 436 and lifted an American record total of 1,152½ pounds for the three Olympic lifts. There was no question. When Hoffman found that I was ready for the Russian trip, I was on my way, uniform or not.

At that time, a successful weightlifter of my build and size was uncommon. The Olympic lifts require speed, agility, coordination, and finesse as well as strength. Even though there had been many powerful lifters in the past, they had not possessed these extra qualities to proficiently perform in the overhead maneuvers; they were only able to do the feats such as lifting large stationary objects. I was well over one hundred pounds heavier than Schemansky, so in no way could his uniform have been appropriate for me.

When the team posed for pictures, there I stood in my street clothes, looking totally out of place, twice the width of any of the other guys, and listed as the new national champion. There was no time for reveling in the spotlight. We were soon off for Russia.

We drove all night to New York, where we boarded a plane for Helsinki, the first stop. Pan American Airlines personnel kindly gave me two seats. This trip was a real thrill for me. I had seldom been far from the Georgia and Tennessee hills, except for brief jaunts to meets in a few big cities. I couldn't wait to see Moscow. It was June 1955; I was determined to break and reset records everywhere we went.

The next day we flew to Leningrad for lunch and then left on a Russian airliner for Moscow. We landed at night and spotlights lit up the plane.

Somehow I was chosen to deplane first, and I guess I was quite a sight for the Russians. I don't know what they expected, but I'm sure I wasn't it. I am certain they had never before seen an athlete like me. I filled the doorway as I walked briskly out and down the steps. We were the first nondignitary delegation from America to visit Moscow after World War II, and we were given a royal welcome. Music and the smell of flowers filled the night air, and the handshakes wouldn't quit. Flashbulbs popped and movie cameras hummed.

The lifters in the various weight classes greeted one another excitedly and exchanged information relating to weights they had achieved by writing with chalk on their palms. I had lifted more than any of them, but since I was unknown, there was no one with whom to talk. There I stood, huge and lonely, a bouquet of roses in my fist.

To the Russians, I must have looked like a mascot. I didn't fit in. We were minus a featherweight lifter and I'm sure that, coupled with Schemansky's injury, convinced the Russians I was simply a last-minute fill-in. Indeed I was.

We were given souvenir gifts and then whisked off to hotels in limos. Immediately, it became evident to me that I was not being taken seriously. First, the Russian lifters were disappointed that Schemansky had not been able to come. The Americans who had befriended the Russians in other international competitions explained the problems and told the Russians through interpreters that I was the replacement. I could tell by the looks on the faces of the Russian coaches and lifters that they were not impressed with this unknown fat man. However, hadn't they heard I had broken Schemansky's record?

My hip still bothered me from the auto accident, so I couldn't walk far at one stretch. The Russians wanted to show us their city, and it was all very intriguing, but I had to stop and rest often. I wished they had driven us or called a taxi, and sometimes I just begged off from another walking tour. I could tell they didn't understand, assuming I was too fat to be mobile. I could hardly wait until the competition, but we had three days of exciting sight-seeing (and walking) to do first. At times I thought they were trying to walk the competitive spirit right out of us. They were used to walking, and they were going to run us ragged before we started.

I simply wasn't impressing the Russians. They knew (scientifically, I guess) that a short man, unlike a tall man, can never develop the pulling power necessary for the heavyweight lifts. Maybe so, if a short man doesn't work on his diet and training to develop compensating strength or become innovative in technique and methods. Perhaps I could have developed even more pulling power had I been taller, but as it was, I had developed more overall power in every muscle for every lift than anyone in history.

The hospitality was great, and we were treated royally. The Russians wanted us to have their best in training facilities. That made me feel good, and I looked forward to working out in one of their highly regarded weightlifting clubs. When we got there, I saw row after row of lifting platforms with beautiful chrome-plated Olympic-style barbells and chalk boxes on each. My first thought was, *Where is the rest of your training equipment?* I was informed that the Russians were specialists. They didn't go in for bodybuilding or showing off. They were interested in dominating the world competition in the three Olympic lifts, and those three were the only lifts they did in training.

I was incredulous. Many of my diet and training ideas were new and were scoffed at by some Americans, but I could hardly believe lifters as serious as the Russians had never discovered what seemed so obvious to me. I had learned a great deal from Bob Peoples, but other secrets were natural outgrowths of daily training. I had concluded that my only edge in international competition would be my determination to train longer and harder than anyone else. Now I was learning differently. Though the Russians were training just as long and hard (and being subsidized), they were not training properly, as I saw it.

My style was to train enough in the Olympic lifts to be aware of my limitations and to perfect technique. The key to excelling, I believed, was stimulating my body with what I call assistance lifts. Many of my assistance exercises consisted of variations of the bench press, deep knee bends, and the dead lift. These were the exercises that would add bulk and power to make my entire body strong for the snatch, the clean and jerk, and the press.

I asked the Russians if I could rig up some pieces of equipment for my own makeshift training area. They agreed and gathered around to see what I was up to.

By taping and adjusting, I moved a chinning bar into position; it became my squat rack. This is a device that holds the barbell off the ground so that the lifter can get under it and put it on his shoulders for deep knee bends. When the Russians saw me loading their beautiful Olympic bar with seven hundred pounds of weights, they chided me a bit, concerned that I might bend the bar. They watched in amazement as I worked my leg and back muscles in repetitions of the deep knee bend. It was obvious that they doubted the value of my kooky training methods. They would simply have to be shown.

The next night we went to Gorki Park, a sports amphitheater, where some sixteen thousand enthusiastic Russians gathered in a steady rain for the meet. I was learning something about the importance the Russians place on some of what we consider minor or nonspectator sports. I had never heard of that many fans at a weightlifting meet. I would have been shocked to see half that many on a dry evening.

As our team lined up to be introduced, U.S. Coach Bob Hoffman showed his nervousness. "Why don't you have on a uniform?"

Was he kidding? Where had he been? "How could I have a uniform?" I asked him. "I've never before lifted for my country."

"Then how will you identify yourself with the team?" he asked.

"When they load the barbell, they'll know who I am," I said.

When the team was introduced, my teammates received polite applause. When I stepped forward, there were snickers, giggles, and a few claps. I smiled.

Alexei Medvedev was the leading Russian heavyweight. He was planning to tie the Olympic record in the press. The way the meet worked was simple: The officials added five pounds to the bar every few minutes until one of the contestants stopped them and made his first lift. Psychology was involved because if a lifter waited until his opponent made the first move, he could find himself having to attempt a weight he had never successfully lifted.

The Americans had won two of the six divisions when Medvedev and I squared off. He finally made his move and tried his first lift at a weight in excess of 300 pounds. It was a warm-up for him. He was aiming to make his third lift at just over 330 pounds.

He made it, and the crowd went wild. Their man had done his best ever and had tied a record. They were sure I wouldn't even try, since he had outdone himself. The officials kept adding weights to the bar in five-pound increments, but because of the language barrier and the unusual nature of the meet, there was some confusion as to whether or not I was going to lift.

"Why isn't your man competing?" the Russians asked Hoffman. "Is the meet over? Have we won?"

"How about it?" Hoffman asked me.

"There isn't enough weight on the bar," I said. He relayed the message to the officials. They were amused and the crowd was informed, resulting in smiles and whispers throughout the amphitheater.

"Well, we don't need to continue adding weight to the bar five pounds at a time," the Russians said, smiling. "Just tell us how much you want."

I told them I wanted 402½ pounds, and they all but laughed out loud. The all-time world record by Doug Hepburn of Canada was just over 360 pounds. Hepburn was a specialist who was mediocre in the other two lifts and could never even compete with Schemansky in world competition because his three-lift total was bad. His record in the press was expected to stand for years.

The crowd got a real kick out of my request. Now they were certain I was a clown, a mascot, or some kind of gag. They chuckled and clapped but seemed impatient to leave if the meet was over except for a sideshow. The rain kept coming. The officials had to scamper around behind the curtain to get weights off the practice bar so they would have enough. When they had over 350 on the bar, they apologized for putting on more weight than I could handle, but I insisted on the 402½, and they kept adding weight. Finally, the bar was loaded.

As usual, I dusted my hands with chalk to get a good grip on the bar, and the people seemed to begin realizing I was serious about attempting the ridiculous lift of over forty pounds more than the existing world record.

I lifted the bar to my chest with ease and waited for the official to clap, signifying that I had paused long enough and could attempt to push the bar above my head. The crowd gasped, but as I started to push the bar, I realized I had forgotten to wipe it clean. The rain had made it slick; it began slipping from my hand. I had to move my feet to reposition myself, and this, of course, nullified the lift. I dropped the bar; it thundered to the floor as the judge's red light flashed and the crowd groaned with an "I knew it" note. I had a three-minute wait before my second attempt.

I wiped the bar carefully and rechalked my hands. Then I cleaned the bar to my chest and waited for the judge's signal. With his clap I drove the bar over my head without a quiver, held it there in triumph, and then carefully set it back on the floor. There was dead silence in the park for about ten seconds. I felt like a man at the end of a newscast who says good night, and the camera stays on him. No one, not even my teammates, could believe it. Suddenly the place was in an uproar. Men stood on chairs and shouted; some tossed hats into the air. I learned later that the Russians, who worship physical strength, were screaming, "He's the strongest man who ever lived; he's a wonder of nature!"

An elderly man rushed to the platform with an interpreter and told me, "I can go home and die now. I have seen everything. I have seen the world's greatest feat of strength!"

I went on to set two more world records that night, one in the clean and jerk and one for total pounds lifted. I beat the Russian, who probably ranked third in the world behind Schemansky and me, by a total of over 165 pounds. I could have lifted more in each event, but we were just beginning a long tour, and I wanted to save something for each meet. What a night! As you might guess, I didn't sleep too well.

It was a night of great fulfillment, and even though I was not as close to God as I should have been and later would be, I thank Him for giving me this success.

Paul Anderson, possibly the strongest man in history and certainly the world's strongest man* in his day, was the last American super-heavyweight to win an Olympic gold medal in weightlifting (at Melbourne in 1956) and the last strongman to be a household name in the United States. Lest you think Paul's general prominence is being exaggerated, consider that he was selected by the U.S. State Department for a worldwide goodwill tour (Rader, 1956c) and was featured across the media, from major national magazines to television news to the popular newsreels of the day (Paschall, 1956). Even a quick review will demonstrate what a prominent role the squat played in Paul's dramatic lifting successes.

Paul began weight-training as a 5'9" 190-pound teenage football player looking for a means to improve his performance. Within a short time, by training "almost exclusively" on the squat and drinking "many quarts" of milk a day, Paul soon weighed 275 pounds and was squatting close to 600 pounds (Rader, 1961, p. 20, 21). Shortly thereafter Paul began rewriting the weightlifting record books: With less than two years' training, Paul was approaching world records in the Olympic lifts, challenging Doug Hepburn as a candidate to be called the strongest man in history, and squatting absolutely phenomenal weights. The mere sight of Paul Anderson was enough to impress, as indicated in this report from the 1955 U.S. Senior national Weightlifting Championship:

In this class we had the fabulous Paul Anderson from Toccoa, Georgia, and we do mean fabulous! You should hear the exclamations of amazement from the audience when he first walks out on the [lifting] platform. He is so huge [5'9" tall and 341 pounds] you can hardly believe it and yet he does not appear fat except a little around the waist. His legs, back, arms, and chest are all very hard (Rader, 1955b, p. 28).

To better understand the significance of Paul's progress, let's take a closer look.

The year was 1951, and nineteen-year-old Paul Anderson, who had "used little else but the squat in his early training days" (Rader, 1954, p. 11), burst on the lifting scene: The official world record in the squat was 600 pounds (Lawson, 1956) and suddenly a teenager with less than one year's training was closing in on the mark. In mid-1953 Paul squatted 763 pounds, compared to Doug Hepburn's best of 665 pounds (Paschall, 1954a). By November 1953 Paul squatted 820 pounds (Glossbrenner, 1987). This was the era in which many authorities were calling Doug Hepburn the strongest man who ever lived and the young Paul Anderson, in a tremendous display of fundamental power, was far out-lifting him in the squat. By the mid-1950's Paul was squatting 900 pounds for repetitions. His equipment, rather than his strength, seemed to be the limiting factor (Lawson, 1956). As part of his stage show in the late 1950s Paul squatted with a phenomenal 1,160 pounds several times a night— forget the technological and pharmacological accoutrements of today's powerlifter, Paul didn't even have to warm up (Glossbrennner, 1987).[†]

---

* Titles such as "The World's Strongest Man" have been so abused that we are somewhat reluctant to even raise the subject. Nonetheless, if *any modern claimant* ever deserved such recognition, in our opinion— without question—it is Paul Anderson. This is hardly an isolated opinion. When asked whether he had any doubt *whatsoever* about whether Paul Anderson in his prime was the strongest man in the world, Peary Rader replied, "Absolutely none" (Rader, 1988). This shouldn't be surprising, since Peary often called Paul the "strongest man who ever lived" (Rader, 1969, p. 12).

† Paul Anderson's feats under the squat bar transcend any analysis at the level of mere athletic performance, no matter how many superlatives are used. They dramatically demonstrate the formidable psychological process of true leadership (Strossen, 1988a,b).

Randall J. Strossen, Ph.D., *SUPER SQUATS: How to Gain 30 Pounds of Muscle in 6 Weeks*

5

In Russia "at the Right Time"

We have all heard the expression "being in the right place at the right time." This is exactly what happened to me in Moscow. I was primed and ready to demonstrate my strength before the Russian people, and because of the uniqueness of the trip and the times, sports enthusiasts throughout the world were focusing their eyes on Moscow that evening. By the next day, sports fans who could read a newspaper, watch television, or hear a radio anywhere in the world knew the name Paul Anderson. If being in the right place at the right time occurs only once in a lifetime, certainly this was my moment. Such opportunities very rarely present themselves, and our main obligation is to be prepared to take full advantage of them.

My instant popularity in Russia and the rest of the world was incredible to me. Because the visit of American athletes was a major news story throughout the world, and I was virtually unknown until that night in Moscow, my feat was televised around the world.

I know now that God had a hand in this. If I had been the world record holder before the Russian trip, my breaking records there would have been expected. The story would have been the visit, not my surprise achievement, which was featured as one of the all-time great moments in sports history. God was giving me a platform of worldwide notoriety that would, in later years, earn me the right to be heard by thousands of people.

How I wish I had been a Christian then. In the New Testament, the Apostle Paul talks about his "thorn in the flesh" (2 Corinthians 12:7). It is not exactly clear what his ailment was, or even whether it was physical or mental. I am aware of my thorn in the flesh. I know I should put it behind me and not live in the past, but until the day I die I will wonder what God might have been able to do through my witness if I had been ready to speak for Him in Russia in 1955.

Happily for me, world records and overnight successes are not quickly forgotten; for years the fame from that and subsequent trips continued to open doors for my Christian witness. I regret that I was not prepared then to capitalize upon it. Because of this, after I came to Christ, I made it a point never to pass up a chance to witness.

If a man can lift more than 400 pounds in the press, he should be able to lift 450 in the clean and jerk. I could have done it that night in Moscow, but Bob Hoffman cautioned me to do just 427. That was a new record by 25 pounds, and he rightly advised me to begin breaking records at a slower pace. It was fine to exceed other people's records by 25 pounds, as long as I didn't break my own records by that much. The day would come when I would be unable to demolish my own records that impressively. Knowing I was capable of lifting another 25 or so pounds more than I was lifting, plus the fact that what I was lifting was still 25 to 40 pounds more than anyone else had ever done, gave me great personal satisfaction. There was no pressure, so I was relaxed and as a result performed my best.

When the tour became tiring and the food was insufficient either in quantity or protein, I didn't worry about lifting the maximum amount of which I was capable. I simply put enough weight on the bar to totally humiliate the opposition, maybe break my world record by a pound or two, and handle it easily in one attempt. That preserved my strength and left plenty of room for more record breaking at later dates.

In Leningrad, we were received with much the same fanfare, and we had a great time. Here, the Russians tried to give us a bit of culture, certain that we were country clods who had never been exposed to the theater or good music. It happened to be somewhat true, especially of me, but I wasn't about to admit it to them.

I was excited about returning to America because I had come to appreciate our way of life more than ever. The Russians seemed to constantly put down capitalism and the free-enterprise system. I thoroughly enjoyed deflating their balloons.

At a beautiful theater in Leningrad, we saw a terrific production of *Swan Lake*. During intermission I found a seat in a corner of the lobby where I could stretch my legs. Immediately I was surrounded by the Russian press. "I'll bet you've never seen anything like this before," a reporter offered through an interpreter.

"Yeah," I replied. "I saw it not too long ago on television." Actually, I had seen only a short portion but thoroughly enjoyed it. I had grown up in a music-oriented home. My sister, Dorothy, became a concert pianist and had the opportunity to go to the Juilliard School of Music but chose to marry and have a family instead. Because of her influence, I was fairly well educated in the classics. Now here I was, telling the Russians I had seen *Swan Lake* on television, giving the impression that what I had seen was as good as the great performance the Russian dance troupe was giving.

"Oh, you can't appreciate *Swan Lake* on a small set," the interpreter said. "You can't grasp its greatness."

"American television screens are big," I fired back defensively.

"How big are they?" the reporters asked almost in unison, edging closer for this secret tidbit from the other side of the Iron Curtain.

"About this big," I said, holding my arms about three feet square in a ridiculous exaggeration.

"Why would they make televisions that big," they asked, "and how?"

"I don't know how," I said. "However, they make them bigger and better all the time because of our free-enterprise system." Now they were really puzzled—and interested. "When one manufacturer offers a TV set to the public, another independent manufacturer has the right to improve upon it. He will make it bigger and better, and then another independent manufacturer will make his bigger and better. Each manufacturer is making the set bigger and better and selling it cheaper to get his share of the business. Because of this, we have the best in quality at the best prices."

One of the Russians thought that sounded like a pretty good deal, and he nodded as I spoke. His comrades noticed and stared him down; he quickly regained his composure. I had never given much thought to our American free-enterprise system until this occasion, when I felt I had to come to its defense. A seed was planted that night and grew through the years as I hailed our free-market way of trade and individual achievement in many of my exhibitions.

During the next couple of weeks, we visited major cities in the Far East. I discovered Montezuma's Revenge, Baghdad Belly, or whatever you want to call it. I enjoyed my first world tour, but

I lived on soft drinks and what I considered "safe" American-type foods. It was great to be famous, but I longed to return home to my mother's cooking. I lost about twenty pounds on the trip.

Iran, Iraq, Egypt, and Lebanon were delightful and hospitable places, and some of the rulers of those countries requested command performances by the new world record holder. I have never been a modest "clod kicker": a person who becomes the best at what he does, but when people ask him about it he just kicks the dirt and says, "Aw, shucks," and blames it on luck. I was the world record holder because I had worked and sacrificed. I could do much better, and I told anyone who wanted to know. I don't regret that.

In Baghdad, I met a missionary who had attended Toccoa Falls Institute, a Bible school in my hometown. It was good to talk with someone from home, but when he asked about my spiritual state, I was quick to tell him what a great Christian family I came from and that I was a member of a solid church back home. I never did let him get to the point of asking me whether or not I knew Christ as my Savior and Lord. I knew enough through my family and church to know that there comes a time in a man's life when he must decide what he will do about Jesus Christ. Will he admit his sin, ask Christ to forgive and cleanse him and become the Lord of his life, or will he do his own thing? My decision was to ignore the issue. I didn't want anything messing up my life. Everything was going just fine, and I wasn't such a bad guy anyway. I had never been involved in what anyone would call gross sin.

Oh, I was proud and self-centered; I suppose I battled jealousy, lust, and other temptations now and then, but I didn't want to be bothered with God. I didn't realize He wanted only His best for me. He wouldn't have messed up my life; He would have enhanced it. I would learn that later. For now, I was content to fake out the missionary and say just enough to make Christians think I was one of them.

On the day we returned to what was then Idlewild Airport in New York, I was too late for my plane to Atlanta. I had no idea that a gigantic parade had been planned to escort me from Atlanta to Toccoa. The Little Leaguers of Toccoa were in Atlanta, all decked out in their uniforms, along with the local civic clubs, men's groups, politicians, and everybody who was anybody on the local or state scene.

Ironically, Bob Hope was aboard the plane I was supposed to have been on. I have never met him, but I have a soft spot in my heart for him because of that day in 1955 when he entertained the crowd that had gathered to welcome me. When he found out who the crowd was waiting for, he quipped, "The plane was having trouble taking off, so Paul volunteered to get out and push us off. He'll be along on the next plane."

As it turned out, I didn't arrive until late that night, and the parade had already left for a big celebration in Toccoa. If I had known I was expected at a specific time, I probably would have found a way to arrive at the airport earlier. Later on, the honors poured in. I was given a key to the city and several trophies and plaques. Also, I was bombarded with requests for pictures and interviews.

I didn't let the publicity and notoriety interfere with my training; instead, I became more dedicated than ever. The success I had achieved would focus attention on me, and I wanted to keep improving. I worked myself mercilessly, adding body weight and lifting poundage, planning for the world championships in Munich just two months away.

Before the October 1955 World Games, I turned down several requests to speak and perform because I knew I would have plenty of opportunities after officially taking the championship.

Though my new records were accurate and confirmed by officials in both the United States and Russia, I wasn't officially the world champion yet. At the World Games, I would make everything official, including my personal domination of the sport.

The team left for Germany about a week after my story appeared in the *Saturday Evening Post*. If I wasn't a national celebrity before that 5-million-circulation issue appeared, I was from then on. I could have stayed home and accepted enough television appearances to keep me going for years, but I couldn't accept money from TV sports appearances so long as I was an amateur (especially as a member of the Amateur Athletic Union, which was, and still is, excessively restrictive in that way). There was no way I would jeopardize my amateur standing at that time. Not until I had won the Olympic Gold Medal in Melbourne, Australia, in 1956 would I entertain such an idea. Maybe after that I might consider becoming a professional. However, I didn't even want to start thinking about the Olympics, at least not until after the 1955 World Championships were out of the way.

We wanted to be sure we could get used to the food and water in Germany and become thoroughly acclimated to the local environment before the competition, so we were in Munich for about a month of training before the championships. I was stronger than ever. I lifted 320 pounds in the snatch, 410 pounds in the press, and 400 pounds in the clean and jerk. The press and total were both world records, and again, I could have done better (the clean and jerk is the easiest; I lifted just enough to win). There were many meets to come that year, and I was continuing to heed Bob Hoffman's advice about breaking records at a slower pace.

When I returned to the States, my real troubles with the AAU began. It seemed that every time I wanted to do anything, I had to clear it with them. It got to be frustrating. We amateurs had to be careful not to have our pictures taken with professionals, or we would lose our amateur standing. We couldn't take money for any reason. Even when I bought a Cadillac with my own money, I came under close scrutiny; the AAU insinuated I had made some money illegally somehow, but it simply wasn't true. I needed a large car, so I bought it.

Once I was invited to appear with Steve Allen, the original host of NBC's "Tonight Show." I explained that I could accept no payment, but I would enjoy being his guest. The AAU asked Allen if the show were sponsored. He replied that dozens of products were presented on the show but promised not to pay me. The AAU nixed the idea anyway. I could hardly believe it.

Another AAU fiasco centered around the *Post* magazine story. The AAU informed me that since the magazine advertised the story, I would have to sue the publishing company to remain an amateur. As an afterthought, the AAU mentioned that any and all monies I won in such a suit were to be turned over to the Union if I were to remain an amateur. I thought it was ludicrous, and a lawyer friend agreed. It was eventually forgotten. I decided I would take the AAU seriously only long enough to qualify for the Olympics. After that, I would turn pro. I was tired of these shenanigans.

I was offered a public relations job with the Georgia Game and Fish Department, which would afford me the opportunity to speak and make appearances without jeopardizing my amateur standing. The job began late in 1955 when I returned from a goodwill trip to the Far East for the State Department. I was thankful to return home; after what I did to a Beirut baggage handler, it's a wonder I wasn't held for ransom.

It was not uncommon for foreigners to confront me in airports and involve me in tugs-of-war or wrist-wrestling matches, so I thought nothing of it when a baggage handler placed his elbow on the counter and gestured to me with his hand. His middle finger was curled out, and he was challenging me to a pulling match.

I didn't recognize it as a challenge to a finger pull. To me, it was the same gesture we used in high school when we wanted to twist fingers. We would interlock middle fingers and twist until one of us gave up. I was so strong that usually I allowed my buddies to grip my finger with their whole hand, but this guy in Beirut looked pretty husky. I figured I needed to give it all I had. If he was brave enough to challenge the world's champion weightlifter, maybe he had some strength.

I grabbed his middle finger with mine and gave it a ferocious twist, which broke the bone and tore the knuckle from its socket. He ran off screaming, and my teammate explained to me that in Lebanon finger *pulling,* not finger *twisting,* is the game. I guess he didn't report me, because I got out of the country without incident.

In December 1955, I was named the Georgia Male Athlete of the Year by the *Atlanta Constitution,* which called me the strongest man since Samson, a world figure, and a goodwill ambassador. After the dismal, injury-ridden year before, 1955 had been one I would never forget.

But 1956 was an Olympic year. The gold medal could make all my other medals, records, and achievements pale in comparison. I wanted it. However, I would get more than I bargained for in Melbourne. The Olympics would be a life-changing experience for me.

6
Miracle in Melbourne

Somehow the Amateur Athletic Union realized I was doing more for it than it was for me and loosened its policy a bit, allowing me to make some television appearances. I appeared on "I've Got a Secret," "The George Gobel Show," and some others, and it made for quite a busy year for me. I had to eat more and work harder to keep my body weight up because all the traveling and work for the state of Georgia made it difficult to stay in shape.

I worked out as often as I could, gave a few demonstrations, and even entered some contests. With everything else I had to do, I was surprised to find myself stronger than ever. I weighed well over 350 pounds; my neck size was 24 inches; my biceps were over 24 inches; my chest, 58; my thighs were 36 inches, bigger than most men's waists. With 900 pounds on my back, I could squat three times. The Olympic trials in October and the games in November would be a breeze.

By the middle of the year I had lifted, in competition, a total of 1,175 pounds for the three Olympic lifts. In individual lifts, I had bests of 440 pounds in the clean and jerk, 408 in the press, and 335 in the snatch, for a total of 1,183. I knew I could do better, and I figured I would during the Olympic Games.

There was no one within one hundred pounds of me in total lifts. I was not only rewriting the record books but I was also discouraging other competitors. Men who were doing better than the old world records were still one hundred pounds away from my lifts. It was a matter of going through the motions in the California Olympic trials in October. I qualified by lifting much less than my capacity because there was so little competition. I won easily with weights lighter than I used for warming up.

When the team arrived in Melbourne, eighteen days before the lifting competition, I was beginning to feel a bit feverish and unsteady; I couldn't pinpoint the reason. I just wasn't comfortable; I didn't feel as if I had a stomach flu or a digestive problem. I wasn't sure what it was, but I was certain that it would take care of itself. However, it didn't.

The newspapers in Australia carried front-page pictures of me with captions that implied I simply had to go to the stadium and pick up my medal—after, of course, routinely picking up enough weights to earn it. They considered my winning a foregone conclusion. The second-best lifter in the world was probably the Russian Medvedev, whom I had beaten by 165 pounds in Moscow. He had greatly improved, as I had, but I was still ahead of him by at least 100 pounds in total lifts. The Russians had decided not to enter him; the only way I could lose was to break a bone or become too sick to perform to the best of my ability.

Less than two weeks before the competition, I woke up in the middle of the night burning with fever. I did not have time to be sick; I needed every day for training. I did not want merely to win the gold medal, as thrilling as that would be. I wanted Olympic records that would stand for ages.

I tried working out in spite of my fever but finally decided I'd better see a doctor. I had to get this thing licked and get back to business. My temperature was 104 degrees and I was sent to the infirmary, where nurses shot me full of antibiotics. However, for twelve days the fever raged, and there was constant talk of sending me back to the States. No one could determine what was wrong. All that doctors and nurses could do was treat me symptomatically.

The United States officials tried to keep my illness a secret, but word leaked out. The other thirty or so heavyweights were encouraged by the news. It wasn't that they had anything against me, but they had come to fight for second place, and here was their chance to go for the gold. I courageously fought against the illness, though it frightened me. At first I was afraid I was going to die; then I was afraid I wouldn't!

I refused to be sent back to the States. As long as there was a chance of recovering in time to lift, I knew I could win. I told myself that Paul Anderson *sick* was better than anyone else in the world *healthy*. I know how egotistical that sounds, but it was true. Even if I were down seventy-five pounds in total lifting, I could still win.

However, things looked more doubtful each day. Finally, three days before the competition, the doctors gave me the bad news: "You will not be able to lift. We cannot allow a man in your condition to compete."

I was crushed. The Olympics were to be icing on the cake. I felt I deserved the gold. It was only right that the world record holder, the greatest weightlifter of all time, should also be the Olympic champion and help his team take the crown. I wanted what was mine. I asked the doctors to postpone their decision until the last instant. They agreed but insisted that, if they felt I should not lift, they would go to the Olympic Committee with the decision. This gave me some hope.

I knew I was in no shape to lift, but my heart overruled my head. I wanted so badly to compete for the gold medal that I decided to take my health into my own hands. Just as I wouldn't recommend cutting the cast off a broken wrist, as I had done in 1954, I don't recommend what I did late in 1956 either, but I did it.

Without the doctors' consent I put myself on four aspirins every three hours. I had lost more than thirty pounds in twelve days, felt miserable, and was turning yellow. Doctors had not been able to make me better, so I found the aspirins when no one was around and began taking them. By the next morning the aspirins had brought my fever down.

When word of my lower temperature reached the doctors, they asked how I felt. Much better, I told them. I couldn't tell whether or not they believed me, but I kept taking the aspirins.

By the morning of the day I was scheduled to lift, November 25, 1956, my temperature was nearly normal, but only because it was being artificially controlled by the aspirins. I did everything I could to make my physicians believe I was recovering. Finally, these concerned professionals said they would not forbid my competing if I would agree to take all responsibility. It was as good as done.

I looked and felt terrible. I weighed in at only 304 pounds and appeared gaunt compared with the 340 competing weight I had settled on for the Olympics. The heavyweights were supposed to lift at 8:00 P.M., but when I arrived it was obvious that the meet was far behind schedule. By eight o'clock the middle heavyweights had hardly begun. It took nearly an hour for each weight class, with every contestant getting three attempts on each lift. I was dressed, but I didn't warm up. I didn't even think about warming up until nearly midnight, when it appeared the heavyweights wouldn't lift until 1:00 A.M. By that time, the effects of my last aspirins had worn off, and my body was getting its revenge for the hours of artificial relief. The fever returned and was even worse than before. I will never know how high it was, but it wouldn't have surprised me to find it was pushing 106 degrees.

My face burned yellow and red. I perspired and shivered. I talked to no one. I bided my time, waiting for my chance to lift for the gold. With each passing minute, my strength was drained by the fever and an inner ear infection. I couldn't even walk without getting dizzy, and balance is so important when trying to press hundreds of pounds overhead. I was frightened and nearly delirious. I would lift if it killed me, and it almost did.

By 1:00 A.M. my raw throat itched and stung. I took off my sweat suit and made my way to the lifting platform. I came close to collapsing and asked myself, *What am I doing here?* However, I was being introduced. I chose only a warm-up weight for my first attempt in the press. I wanted to grab it and press it to give myself a feel for the bar.

When I cleaned the bar to my chest, I could hardly believe how heavy it seemed. I pressed it and was given credit for a valid lift. When I increased the weights for my next two attempts, there was no making them. I was horrified. I couldn't relate to the feeling of being behind in competition. In the press, I had lifted only my warm-up weight, and as impressive as it was, it would not win a gold medal.

By 2:00 A.M. I could barely see. I was so glad I had decided to lift a lighter weight than usual in the press. Otherwise, I might have been eliminated with no lift in the press. I wouldn't have been able to face that. The other lifters realized things weren't right for me. They knew I was either in terrible condition or playing a game. It would not have surprised them to find I could do nearly five hundred pounds in the clean and jerk and was saving a dramatic winning lift for the last instant. I could clean and jerk nearly five hundred pounds in practice, and I had been toying with the idea of attempting it in the Olympics, but not on this day. No way! It would be all I could do to remain conscious for the next two events. If I could get through the meet without totally humiliating myself, maybe I would be credited with not being a quitter. I could come back one day and break more records. But right now, I just needed to survive.

I still held out a faint hope that I could make up for my dismal press with better lifts in the snatch and the clean and jerk.

I used the same strategy in the snatch. I started with a weight I knew I could handle in order to keep myself in the competition; I was hoping to use one of my two remaining lifts in that event to pick up some total poundage. I snatched the bar from the floor, only to stagger and nearly drop it before somehow driving it overhead. I shook my head in disbelief. It was a "nothing" weight for me, child's play. There were days when I might not even have started with a weight that light for practice. But I had made it and was assured of staying in the competition. However, I needed a better lift in one of my next two attempts to put myself in good standing going into the clean and jerk.

When I failed at my next two attempts at slightly heavier weights in the snatch, I realized I was going into the clean and jerk behind in both initial events. It hit me between the eyes that I was going to lose. I had never before trailed in even one event. There had never been a meet in which I had to lift so much more than the others in the last event to pull the victory out of the fire. Now I was faced with just that prospect. The other lifters were so psyched up they could hardly wait to lift. They were outdoing themselves, beating their personal records with each lift. The crowd was going wild. I was exhausted. There was no reason for me to think I could do any better in the third event than I had done in the first two.

I was determined to neither give up nor go for second place. I decided I might as well go out trying. I had nearly killed myself to stay in the competition, even with the relatively light weights I had lifted. I went to a little room behind the platform to rest and asked an Australian aide to please wake me when it was my turn to lift. I would not warm up. I would do nothing but sleep. I was not certain I would even be able to rise from the cot when my Aussie friend tried to wake me. I was pulling out all the stops. I would see it through to the end. I tried praying, but my heart had grown cold from years of ignoring God, so I just dozed off in fitful sleep, waking every few moments and wondering if the Aussie had already tried to wake me.

One thing I dreaded more than lifting again: not lifting again. I was miserable, close to tears, and totally spent.

Finally the Aussie shook me. It was half-past three in the morning, now November 26. "I'm very sorry to have to tell you this," he began, "but to win you will have to lift an Olympic record four hundred fourteen and a half pounds to make up for your first two lifts. That will tie Selvetti at a total of one thousand, one hundred two pounds and give you the victory." Argentina's Humberto Selvetti had weighed in at 316 pounds, and since I was now twelve pounds lighter, under Olympic rules I would get the gold.

I looked at the Aussie with glazed eyes, nodding slowly. Before I became ill, 414½ pounds in the clean and jerk would have been a piece of cake. I had lifted 440 in competition and nearly 500 in practice. My three-lift total had been 1,175 in one meet, and now I was being advised that all I had to lift was 1,102. Yet in my condition, it was impossible to reach that total. What should I do—try it and make a fool of myself, or go for a lighter weight and take a lesser medal or possibly no medal at all?

I thought long and hard. I ached all over. I finally decided that if I could lift anything, I could lift the 414½. There would be no point in lifting anything less. I had not come to lose. I had come to win. I shook myself from the cot and inched my way to the platform. I asked for 414½ pounds to be placed on the bar, and the officials loaded it without comment. The hall was quiet. The crowd had remained. The other lifters had mixed feelings. They looked on sympathetically, yet hopefully.

The Argentinean who would win the gold if I failed was being encouraged by Russian coaches, no less. They had not entered their heavyweight, choosing to place two men in a different weight class instead; they had steered Medvedev away from me, knowing that he stood no chance. If I finished any lower than first place in my weight class, they would win the team championship, which naturally gave the Russians an interest in the Argentinean.

If anything, I felt worse after the nap than I had before. In my first attempt, I lifted the bar from the floor to my chest and grimaced. There was no way. It was too heavy. I had nothing left. My mind and my body would not react simultaneously. I lurched in an attempt to drive the bar overhead but never got it past my chin. The bar crashed to the floor, and the room was silent except for the echo.

My teammates rushed to surround me, slapping me on the back. "Come on, Paul!" they shouted. "We know you can do it. Never say die!" It encouraged me, but I was burning up. If there was a chance for me to score, I owed it to the team to try. I had three minutes of rest between attempts. Their encouragement made me hopeful. Suddenly it was time to lift again.

I rushed to the bar and pulled it to my chest. My enthusiasm was gone immediately. If anything, it was heavier than before. I moaned in defeat as I tried to stiffen beneath the bar and shake it overhead. I failed more miserably than the first time. The bar rumbled to the floor and I stomped away, bitterly disappointed. I had one more try. I was mad, hurt, and desperate; I reasoned that no amount of psyching could enable me to lift that bar. I had been defeated.

I knew my last lift would be a futile charade, and I wondered if I should concede defeat. I wasn't sure I could even get it to my chest one more time. There was no way I was going to lift that weight over my head, but at least I had to try. I waved my teammates away as they rushed again to encourage me. I don't think they ever gave up on me. They couldn't imagine my not pulling it out of the fire for them. I had three minutes to get myself together.

As I contemplated the possibilities of losing, my mind raced. What would others think of me? I especially considered the feelings of my parents and friends. What would life be like for a loser? I had never experienced the bitter taste of defeat. I had been congratulated by the president and international heads of state. I had been called a wonder of nature, the strongest man in the world. I had never lost a fight, a race, even an argument. Losing was not in my vocabulary. The only losses I had ever suffered had come in the last two hours when I found myself trailing in individual events.

I used my officially allotted rest period of three minutes to walk up a long, dark corridor; I felt as if God were reminding me of everything He had ever done for me. He had made me what I was. Everything I had accomplished had been because He had let me survive Bright's disease as a child. He had given me loving Christian parents. In spite of His countless blessings, I had ignored Him.

It was impossible for me to pray. I tried twice, but my heart had been hardened by ignoring Him for so long that I couldn't be sincere with Him. At this lowest point in my life, a point to which many people must come before they realize a need for God, I recognized how unworthy I was of His love. I returned for my third attempt at the lift.

The arena was silent. I chalked up. When I pulled the weight to my chest in the cleaning motion, I knew immediately that it was futile. I couldn't put it overhead. Now I was desperate. In a split second, I found I could be sincere with God.

As quickly as the words could race through my heart and mind, I told God I was aware that He had given me everything, and I had returned nothing. *I want to be part of Your kingdom, and from here on out, I'm making a real commitment.*

Then I realized my immediate need. *I'm not trying to make a deal, God, but I must have Your help to get this weight overhead.* At last I had made the commitment I should have made years earlier. I bent my knees slightly for the momentum to push the weight. The bar had already stayed on my chest four to five seconds, an unusually long time for that amount of weight. I gave the final push.

I drove the bar overhead, and it stayed.

The crowd went wild as I returned the bar to the floor. I had suddenly become the Olympic gold medalist! We had won, and 1,102 was a total poundage record for Olympic competition. My smile was not as much for the joy of victory or the relief that the ordeal was over but for my new relationship with Christ. After years of indifference, I was His.

Yes, I had driven the 414½ pounds overhead and had won the gold medal—the last United States heavyweight lifter to do so since that time, as it has turned out. I had lifted far more in the past and would lift much more in the future. The poundage was not important. Even the gold medal was not the real prize. A far greater miracle had occurred. What I really won was not an Olympic championship measured by the poundages of man but the strength of God's Holy Spirit. I had finally learned that His strength would not be diluted by the diseases of my vulnerable flesh-and-bone structure.

Following the victory, I was anxious to return to the United States and fully recuperate from my illness. A professional career awaited me, as well as whatever mission my Lord might call me to fulfill. I was ready.

Dramatic Triumph

Melbourne, Australia—Paul Anderson of Toccoa, Ga., won the heavyweight weightlifting event in an epic three-hour test of strength with Argentina's Humberto Selvetti. Anderson's triumph, one of the most dramatic in Olympic history, was finally achieved at 3:00 A.M., Melbourne time.

The 23-year-old, 304-pound Anderson won only because he was the smaller man.

With an awed crowd looking on at the Melbourne exhibition hall, the two strong men tied with a total lift of 1,102 pounds. Anderson finally received the gold medal under the Olympic weightlifting rules because Selvetti weighed in officially at 316 pounds—12 more than the United States world record holder.

The drama reached a peak when Anderson, straining every muscle in his huge body, his 52½-inch chest fairly bursting, set an Olympic record of 414.5 pounds in the jerk to equal Selvetti's total lift.

The New York Times, November 27, 1956

7
The Real Battle

I never did find out exactly what had been wrong with me to cause such a fever, but the gold medal and a few days of rest seemed to cure it quickly. I was still weak and tired when I stepped joyfully on home soil once again, but being back in the States gave me a lift. The first thing I wanted to do was to be open to God's leading in my life. There just had to be something specific He wanted me to do with my abilities. It wasn't long before I knew, but it was some time before I did it.

After the Olympics, which millions of Americans had viewed on television, I was one of the more recognizable people in the country and one of the best-known athletes in the world. Back then, and up until just a few years ago, even a "somebody" was a "nobody" until he had been on "The Ed Sullivan Show." My notoriety became fixed after three appearances on that variety program. I was known everywhere and was extended many more invitations than I could accept. These ventures altered my status from amateur to professional, which opened many doors for me to pursue fame and fortune as one of history's best-known professional strong men.

It was good to be free of the restrictions, and I had no more amateur ambitions anyway. There was no sense in preparing for the 1960 Olympics if it meant four years of poverty. With a couple of TV shows here and some exhibitions there, I became a full-fledged professional strong man.

It was then that I began to realize what God would require of me after my Melbourne commitment. I gave many lifting demonstrations at detention homes and prisons; I began to develop a deep concern for young people. I realized that without a good environment and a loving family, I could easily have become a troubled young man. What really hit me was that the men in the prisons didn't look like the gangsters in the movies. Many of them were young men. They could have been the kids next door, and many were.

The idea came slowly at first, but when it all started to come together, I could hardly wait. I would use my abilities to make money and start a home for troubled and homeless young people. After having traveled as a goodwill ambassador for the State Department, I knew I had something to offer as a patriotic example. I was also beginning to develop strong opinions about the value of discipline and hard work. If I could be a "father" to some of these products of broken homes, perhaps they would become productive citizens rather than jail statistics. I also knew that God would have me share with them His life-changing Gospel. What a contrast. Rather than becoming convicts, they could become Christians and mature into solid citizens.

Strangely enough, shortly after I made this decision, Satan had me right where he wanted me. Here I was with a noble and, indeed, God-given mission, yet Satan was able to attack. When people or groups heard about my plans, they thought it was the most wonderful goal a man in his early twenties could pursue. That made me increasingly proud, and pride became a big problem in my life.

People who before had debated whether or not they could

afford to book me were now convinced that a project of this sort was certainly worth their money. I called the project the Paul Anderson Youth Foundation and went about raising money for it. It was not as difficult as I thought it might be. America had come to worship strength. Whether I was carrying a donkey up a hill or lifting several grown men on a platform, people flocked to watch, and more invitations poured in.

With my fame and success, I allowed the Youth Foundation to become lost in the shuffle. I was still talking about it and raising money for it; but with only a small amount of personal savings to draw on, I was using much of the income for travel and other needs. Satan was shrewdly blurring the vision God had given me, and the Youth Home was always somewhere way out there in the future. Several times I could have taken a step of faith, pushed harder for funds, and bought some land and made a move to care for some floundering youths, but I was too caught up in activities that Satan convinced me were necessary to raise funds.

I played a part in a Hollywood movie, just for money for the Youth Home. I did some boxing and did well, just for money for the Youth Home. I pro wrestled for a time, again doing well, just for money for the Home. Everything I did in those months was so noble and so right, "just for money for the Home," but the Home itself remained only an idea.

In a nightclub act, I proved my strength was far greater than it had ever been. I never lost sight of my commitment to Christ, but I made the great mistake of taking my eyes off Him. Over the years, I have told audiences that receiving Christ as Savior is only the beginning. A true follower of our Lord must develop himself through daily Bible study and prayer and really make Him Lord of his life. I needed to involve myself with a body of believers who would give me fellowship, training, and counsel, yet all that seemed to take a backseat to my fund-raising efforts for the Youth

Home. I was heady with fame and success, and though the project was still a reality, I began to wonder if I would ever get it going.

I didn't realize that I either had to grow as a Christian or simply wither. There is no middle ground for a child of God. It became apparent to me that I was in trouble. I was like too many church-people today: so busy working for God that they don't have time to worship Him and live for Him.

Ironically, some of my great feats of strength didn't even get me the recognition I deserved. On "The Ed Sullivan Show," I lifted twenty or so chorus girls on a carousel during rehearsal, and I told Sullivan I estimated their total weight to be about twenty-seven hundred pounds. During the live show, I lifted more people, most of them grown men, in an approximate total of nearly five thousand pounds. Yet, based on my statement during rehearsal, Ed Sullivan announced that I was lifting only twenty-seven hundred pounds.

By June 1957 people had begun to ask: If you are indeed the World's Strongest Man and World and Olympic champion, why aren't you listed in the *Guinness Book of World Records?* French-Canadian Louis Cyr had the record for the most weight ever lifted in any manner by man with the incredible four thousand pounds-plus back lift (crouching under a table loaded with weights and lifting it on his back). His record had stood since before the turn of the century.

I decided to break Cyr's record in my hometown, partly because of the prohibitive cost involved in moving all that weight to another area. I trained long and hard between exhibitions at weightlifting meets and in nightclubs, then invited the proper authorities to Toccoa. I worked with my father to build the platform and lifting table.

We had to know exactly how much the lifting table weighed before the lift, so after we nailed it together, we took it apart and weighed it. (You can imagine how much wood and nails went into a table that would support thousands of pounds of weights. The table itself weighed eighteen hundred pounds.) Then we nailed the table together again.

We weighed each weight as it was added to the table. When the total of weights and the table reached 6,270 pounds, I set myself carefully and squarely beneath it and raised it off the ground, breaking the record by more than a ton.[1]

I did not find the feat extremely difficult, and I was certain I could have lifted more, but there was no reason for it. Since it was two thousand pounds above the previous record, my lift should stand for years. No one else has even attempted it. (Believe it or not, I think I may have lifted more than that record later in a 1971 lift at the Youth Home in Vidalia. A television special was being filmed, and for one shot we loaded a couple of horses and our boys onto the back of a truck. The front end of the truck remained on the ground, and I lifted the rear end, completely loaded, off the ground. I'm fairly certain that the lift was far greater than the 1957 feat, but there was no way to verify it.)

In 1958, I did a lot of training and loafing, always telling myself that when I had the money for the Youth Home I would do more speaking in churches and sharing my faith. But it never quite seemed to work out. In late 1958 and early 1959, I lifted less and less, and my body weight dropped to under 300 pounds. I had been lifting at about 390 but found I had too much bulk in my chest and shoulders to allow the necessary flexibility. So, I laid off from lifting for a while and lost 100 pounds. I stayed in

1. *The Guinness Book of World Records* entry reads: "*Greatest Lift.* The greatest weight ever raised by a human being is 6,270 lbs. in a back lift (weight lifted off trestles) by 364-lb. Paul Anderson (U.S.) (b. 1932), the 1956 Olympic heavyweight champion, at Toccoa, Georgia, on June 12, 1957. (The heaviest Rolls-Royce, the Phantom VI, weighs 5,936 lbs.)"

shape by learning to box and even drummed up enough interest to get myself into nine bouts. I won all but one and was progressing well, but there was little money in it.

The point is that I was running away from my own project. I was doing everything but what I had committed myself to do. I was miserable. Because God's Spirit dwelt in me, I was more sensitive than ever to the time I was wasting. Had I not been a Christian, had I been the same Paul Anderson who had learned to conveniently ignore God, I probably would have sailed right along to become just another money-hungry pro athlete. I believe I was actually more miserable because I had God's Spirit convicting me all the while.

Then God sent a stabilizing influence into my life. I had been casually acquainted with Glenda Garland, for I had been friends with her dad because of our mutual interest in horses. When I saw and talked with her at her uncle's funeral in the early summer of 1959, I suddenly realized that this blue-eyed brunette had grown into the most beautiful young lady I had ever seen. We began dating then, soon became engaged, and married a few months later on September 1.

Having graduated that spring from high school in Tallulah Falls, Georgia, Glenda was ten years my junior but noticeably mature for her years, and a woman with a deep desire to please Christ, to whom she had committed her life. I believe to this day that God sent my wonderful wife, Glenda, into my life to help me grow as a Christian and to be the catalyst I needed in getting the Youth Home started. When I told her my idea of starting a home for troubled youth, she was immediately intrigued.

I soon found myself drifting out of show business and boxing and moving more into the area of school and church engagements. I was speaking out for Christ often and, without any booking agency or special lifting equipment, I found myself with more invitations than I could handle.

I had always had a knack for holding an audience's attention. The lifting would get them on my side (sort of the way you get a mule's attention by clubbing him first with a two-by-four), and then my speaking would keep them with me.

I was asked to do some shopping center, promotional-type appearances, and I accepted them as long as I could witness for Christ as part of my thirty- to forty-minute exhibition. That's what really started my career of combining my weightlifting and Christian witness. I realized that much of my confusion and running around during the late 1950s had been due to my rebelling from the very project that had been so dear to my heart.

For sure God had given it to me, and I felt a burden for troubled youth, but I was a loner. What else could I be? I couldn't understand why the same God who made me a loner would also call me into the service of troubled youth. I would find out, but not until I quit running and jumped into the action.

In 1961, Glenda and I were living in a little motel on the edge of Vidalia, approximately two hundred miles southeast of Atlanta. I had told several people about our hope to find property and start a home for underprivileged children, so it wasn't really a surprise when the sheriff called one night in early October. The mother of two young girls, eight and twelve years of age, had been trying to sell her older daughter into prostitution. When we checked into the situation and determined how rough things were for both girls, we decided it was time to officially begin our Youth Home. They became our first foster children and lived with us right there in the motel. It wasn't an ideal place to begin our ministry, but it was surely a better living situation for the girls than what they had been experiencing. We were on our way at last. I wasn't yet thirty and Glenda wasn't yet twenty, but we soon rented a two-story house in Vidalia and within weeks had girls and boys living with us.

After our Youth Home became well established and we had an opportunity to thoroughly evaluate our effectiveness, we discontinued ministering to girls because we concluded that to serve both sexes and minister effectively to them on one campus was almost impossible. If we should ever be led to work with young ladies, we decided we would set up a separate facility.

Word traveled fast when we began our ministry, and it came to our attention that the juvenile courts had an abundance of needy cases that judges would be glad for us to take under wing. It didn't take long for me to realize that I had not been called to be any fellow's buddy. God had called me to this ministry to be the father figure so sorely needed by teenagers who had never had a father they could respect. I quickly learned that most problem young men had gone astray because their fathers had not given them the necessary discipline and love.

I soon learned that young men appreciated my hollering at them when they should have been toeing the line. They seemed to eat it up. They somehow knew that consistent, fair discipline was a demonstration of love, not hate. They responded to me and wanted me to care enough to yell at them once in a while.

We received no financial help from the county or state for the care of these young people, and little if any aid from the parents. I finally had peace knowing that, though my less than two thousand dollars in savings was going fast, I was doing what God had called me to do, and Glenda was as happy as I was.

How we were going to keep food on the table for ourselves and our eight youngsters was something only God knew. Somehow He would bring in the required financial support.

Astonishing Lifts

As part of a Las Vegas nightclub act, Paul squatted with a barbell loaded with coins weighing 1,000 pounds. If anyone in the audience could squat this contraption, he would win the coins, supposedly worth $10,000. No one ever tried. In an exhibition in Alabama in 1963, Paul Anderson cleaned and pressed 450 pounds, snatched 340 and just missed cleaning 460 for a 1,250-pound total. As part of his training during this time, Paul regularly did sets of 10 reps with over 600 pounds in the squat, and half and quarter squats with 1,200–1,500 pounds.

Paul probably reached his strength peak somewhere in the mid- to late-'60s, although he continued to lift unbelievable poundages up until 1980. He claims his best lifts as follows:

- squat, 1,115 pounds
- bench press, 625 pounds
- deadlift without straps, 780 pounds
- deadlift with special hook attachments, 800 pounds
- clean and press, 485 pounds
- clean and jerk, 485 pounds
- snatch, 375 pounds
- push press, 545 pounds
- back lift, 6,270 pounds
- one-arm dumbbell bent press, 240 pounds 40 times; 300 pounds 11 times

Jeff Everson, "The Strongest Man Who Ever Lived," *Muscle & Fitness*, August 1987

8
Making It Work

In the early months after the establishment of the Paul Anderson Youth Home, most of my speaking engagements took me to local churches, clubs, and schools. After getting our small family off to school, I began driving to area schools and universities for lifting and speaking exhibitions.

I tried to be back home in time for supper with the growing family, but then I was off again for evening appearances, usually not returning to Vidalia until the wee hours of the morning. It was a rough life, one that taxed my endurance, but I loved it because I believed it was an assignment God had given me.

We had no other income in those early years. We used what I earned speaking and lifting to provide room and board for the boys, Glenda, and me. I still tried to work out regularly, but the toll of traveling, worrying, and just plain hustling to make ends meet made it hard to be consistent. Only the Lord's uplifting response to prayer gave me enough strength to carry on.

My body weight, which had sped back into the 350s at the end of my boxing career, began decreasing. The only workouts I could schedule some days were at the exhibitions. Knowing that my speeches and my appeal depended upon my remaining the strongest man in the world, I decided I couldn't let my workouts slip. I was not always able to work out as much as I wanted, but unless there was a crucial barrier, I got in enough powerlifting with some of my more punishing lifts to keep my body weight at a 375-pound minimum and my strength at never less than about 95 percent of maximum. I figured that after a month or so of steady training I would be able to outlift the second strongest man in the world in any lift. That's why I didn't hesitate to allow groups to advertise me as the World's Strongest Man.

These matters, however, were minor compared with problems I began to encounter in connection with our Youth Home. We needed positive direction establishing practical, organizational policies. We were still neither incorporated nor tax-exempt. We didn't know if we wanted to expand to take in five hundred teenagers from the courts or stay with only a few in a more homelike environment. One thing was certain: I needed help in making these decisions. I was running myself into the ground.

We decided we needed a partner. It would have to be a man who had a track record of organizational and financial success. Obviously, he would have to be a Christian and have an understanding of what we were endeavoring to accomplish. He would already be a busy man if he had that much going for him, but I wouldn't be afraid to approach him. We needed just the right person, and when I determined who it might be, I decided to be direct.

The obvious choice was Gerry Achenbach, president and chairman of the board of Piggly Wiggly Southern, a highly successful large grocery chain. Here was a man with a knack for organizing people. With insight and hard work, he had made himself and several other executives wealthy. Naturally, he wondered what I wanted from an association with him.

"I don't even want a salary for my work in connection with the Home," I told him. "If you can just help us raise enough money to run the place for five years, we'll worry about such things later." I am sure he realized right away that personal gain was not my aim. If this had been my goal, a Youth Home certainly wasn't the way to go. He agreed to become a corporate partner with my wife and me (in Georgia, three parties are required to form a corporation), and we immediately began to seek community support.

Gerry Achenbach became chairman of our board, and I remained the principal fund-raiser, while Glenda continued to be mother and bookkeeper, shouldering many other responsibilities as director of the Home while I was on the road.

Meanwhile, a man who owned some property in Vidalia died and his estate was being divided. We rented his house for a year because we had no money to buy it. We fixed it up, cleaning, rebuilding, and painting. Eventually, we bought the buildings and the land. The "Big House," as we call it, is a typical Southern plantation-type structure. It has served as our basic facility and actually has grown to represent the Home's image. As one of the original board members put it, "The big white house makes us look like a home and not an institution."

For many years, I drove day and night to engagements all over the country. Some nights I would sleep just two hours, other nights just one, and some none. Once I left Vidalia at one o'clock in the morning for a 750-mile drive to Shreveport, Louisiana, did a program at a church there, and returned to Vidalia without rest. In those years when I traveled extensively, it was not uncommon for me to put over 100,000 miles per year on my car. At one time we owned a private plane and I flew to many engagements; on more distant trips, I took commercial flights. It took all of this to raise needed funds for the growing ministry we had at the Youth Home. I suppose some thought I was getting a big percentage of the one hundred thousand dollars or so that I raised annually, since I was flying in my own private plane and driving a big car, but in reality I was by this time drawing only a modest salary, and that's still the case. This met the IRS requirements so that my work could continue to support the Home.

It used to bother me when people made snide comments about what appeared to be extravagances in our ministry. I ceased to listen to them much. When we first got a swimming pool for the boys (I took on extra exhibitions for a couple of months and made sure all other expenses were taken care of first in order to build the pool), one man said, "I wish my boys could have a swimming pool."

"You follow me around twenty-four hours a day and do what I do," I said, "and you can give them one."

I got cross-eyed looks because of the expensive car, but I had had enough driving all night in Chevy and Ford stickshifts. I found I could lease a car cheaper than buying, and when a luxury car dealer friend found out what I was paying to lease, he said he would lease me a car at the same price. Now what would you have done if you had been my size and did as much driving as I was doing in those days? I concluded it would be counterproductive to drive anything less than a big car.

In our case, owning a private plane was hardly an extravagance. On the occasions when we could operate and maintain such equipment, I was able to make many more appearances. It was a money-maker, not an expense. I once heard that Dwight L. Moody was on a train with a young preacher who was trying to impress the evangelist with his piety. "I purchased just a day coach ticket," the young man said. "I'm going to sit up all night and save God's money."

Moody stroked his beard. "Young man," he said, "I paid for a sleeper, and tonight I'll sleep and save God's servant." If someone had offered me a jet plane, I would have taken it. God's people don't have to run around in rags as second-class citizens. We represent the King of the Universe. Because He owns it all, we own it all.

Even with the one hundred thousand dollars I would bring in, we counted on donors—and still do, more than ever—to meet our budget. Our life-style is hardly extravagant. In those years, I was on the road speaking five hundred times a year to more high schoolers than any other man, though I would love to have stayed home more with Glenda, our daughter, Paula, God's gift to us in 1966, and our boys. But that was God's way of putting food on the table and enabling us to maintain our ministry to youth and, of course, spread His Word to those who would come to listen to a champion athlete speak.

Our boys, whom we consider family members, are products of broken homes, dysfunctional families, or wards of the court. Most of our young men have offended society in some way. Generally, we find that they are adolescents who have begun to resent authority. More often than not, the father has packed up and vanished, leaving the mother with the responsibility of authority and discipline. I've always believed, with a few exceptions, that it is easier for a man to raise a boy or girl alone than for a mother to do so.

When a mother is put into the role of ultimate authoritarian, problems can develop. She is supposed to be the compassionate one, the balance. She is to support both the discipline of her husband (if she is not a single parent) and the needs of her children, plus run the home. When a child hurts himself, he yells for his mommy, not his daddy. Mama functions as a consoler and a companion. If she must become father as well, she is being stretched past her limit. In many cases, that's where the Paul Anderson Youth Home comes in.

From the start, our first concern has been to give the boys at our Home a Christian witness, which has been strengthened over the years. I have at times been asked if I have led many of our young men to the Lord. No, I haven't. I am the boss. What I say goes. Over the years, I have functioned as the leader, the strong father image most boys who come to us have needed for years. Living with us, they respond with respect and sometimes fear, so other staff personnel usually have the joy of bringing them to Christ; it might not be a valid, self-made decision for Christ on their part if I dealt with them one-on-one.

Through the years I have tried to set a Christian example for the boys. I have counseled them individually and led our fellows in devotions, as well as preaching to them and teaching from the Bible. My role in more recent years has been limited to a large degree because of my health problems, but our boys are still dealt with firmly. (Various illnesses that have plagued my body for more than a decade are dealt with in detail in later chapters.)

Psychiatrists might gasp if they knew how I have treated some of the problem cases. One boy had been prescribed a couple of bottles of tranquilizers. I emptied both except for two pills in each and told him to take those two if he needed them, but I would rather he showed me how long he could get along without them. Weeks later he still carried the pill bottles, both with the two pills remaining.

Another boy was a stutterer. No one had told him to stop and start his statement over when he stuttered. I would interrupt him and say, "Now just stop, slow down, and say what you want to say." I wasn't born yesterday. I know this is supposed to be the worst thing to do; however, the boy knew I loved him. If I didn't, why would I bother trying to correct or help him? His stuttering is now history.

One young man had a complex that caused him to twitch and sling his head to the side, especially when he knew people were watching him. Each time he walked by me he would sling his head to the side when I said hello or even looked at him; every time, I told him to quit it. He finally quit. No one had ever told him to stop. He figured no one cared; maybe no one did.

In the middle sixties, I put 120,000 miles a year on my car. Finally I started booking engagements in clusters so we could fly to more of them, and we purchased a plane in 1969. I first booked churches and athletic banquets and then anything else for evenings. I took invitations in the same area for day appearances. I used no booking agent. When I was scheduled in a certain town, the word generally got around and other requests began pouring in.

Often my day would include a breakfast, a couple of high schools before lunch, a civic club luncheon, a high school and a college in the afternoon, plus a banquet in the evening. I lifted at every meeting.

When I was on the road, Glenda ran the Home. She supervised our fellows and additional staff when we were blessed enough to have help. She still inspects the place with a white glove and insists that her boys present themselves in public looking sharp. If their clothes don't match, she asks them to change. Merely because they are not in a ''natural home'' doesn't mean our young men should dress in discarded attire or be poorly groomed. That would certainly not be conducive to a good self-image.

Glenda provides all of the leadership at the Home and manages the office. She also handles a vast majority of the counseling, interviewing, and performing dozens of other vital necessities. She puts in an average of sixteen hours a day, and besides the business portion of her commitment, she gives personal love and care to each one of our young people, just as though he were her own. Even though she holds the title of assistant director and chief fiscal officer, Glenda really is the director of the Home, as far as her responsibilities are concerned. She never wanted to be on payroll and was not until I became ill.

We are the boys' parents, and as part of our parental duties we buy their clothes. Admittedly, we have contacts with many stores and clothiers and can get good prices. We aren't extravagant, but our young men dress well.

During my traveling days, Glenda kept track of the boys who misbehaved and I dealt with them when I returned. We felt they needed a father figure, a boss, and that was, and still is, Paul Anderson. When a boy did something wrong, he faced punishment—generally physical labor—and he did it until he broke into a sweat. At that point, he was no longer uptight. His will had been broken, and he was ready to talk. This remains our method of discipline.

Our young men have always gone through stages when they arrive to be our family members. In the beginning, they are generally afraid of me but warm up as they get to know me. I make it a practice to joke with each boy occasionally.

From the outset, Glenda and I have asked the boys to address us by our first names, not "Mr. and Mrs. Anderson" or "Mom and Dad," for we want them to reserve these and similar terms for their parents back home. All other adults are addressed by their formal names, and in keeping with Southern custom, boys show respect with "yes, sir" and "yes, ma'am" in their conversations with adults.

Experience early showed us that some boys blame their home life for their problems. Even if this is so, in my talks on forgiveness, I stress that all parents make mistakes. We must be Christlike and forgive parents instead of holding grudges. I explain to the boys that the first step in forgiving others is to receive Jesus Christ as their Savior and Lord and allow the Holy Spirit to forgive them; then wiping out the past difficulties with others will be much easier.

Glenda and I have made it a point to tell our boys right off that we are not interested in the wrongs they have done. When they enter the Paul Anderson Home, it is as if they are starting over, as if they were born today.

"I don't care whether you like me when you leave here," I have always told our fellows. "What I care about is whether you become a productive citizen when you leave." Of course, I really do want them to like me. In my active years, I played football with them and quarterbacked for both teams. We had some great times together.

The boys soon find out that I expect more from them than gratitude, that I want them to do what is right because of themselves, not because of me. I emphasize that they can't do certain things while under our supervision because we love them enough to watch them closely. Over the years, our young men have responded wonderfully. They get the message: we really want the best for them in life.

The ones with whom I have problems are not ones I can't discipline. I can discipline anyone. The challenge isn't to discipline but to motivate.

One of the boys I took in several years ago was fifteen at the time and had been given plenty of discipline but no motivation. He had been involved in a theft; I had noticed him at the Atlanta juvenile hall. He was ironing his own clothes and seemed industrious. I asked about him.

"Oh, you don't want that rascal," his probation officer said. That surprised me, because probation officers usually try to sell me on their cases.

"Why not?"

"He's on his way to prison and is just biding his time here."

"What did he do?"

"He stole a car, and a crummy one at that. It didn't get him three blocks, so he broke into a store at midnight and stole the tools and parts to fix it. When he was caught, he was charged with grand theft—auto, breaking and entering, and burglary."

It sounded serious, but it seemed to me that a youth with enough initiative and knowledge to fix a car could be motivated to be a good boy. We acquired custody, and he eventually became a fine Christian young man.

I am convinced that God has given us wisdom to operate a program that works.

God's Special Arrangement
By Paula Anderson Schaefer

I am a fortunate and special young lady, an extremely priv-
ileged, handpicked child of God. I have been "adopted
twice," first by wonderful earthly parents, and then by Jesus Christ. When I received Him as my Savior, He adopted
me into the family of God. "Having predestinated us unto
the adoption of children by Jesus Christ to himself, according to the good pleasure of his will" (Ephesians 1:5).

Mama and Daddy told me from childhood that I was
adopted, and that made me a special little girl. From earliest
memory, I recall telling my parents that Jesus chose one of
His lady angels in heaven and sent her down to earth to have
me. People always comment about how much my mother
and I resemble each other, so I know the hand of God was
in my adoption. He even went to the finest detail of allowing me to have the same appearance as my mother.

I belong to my parents just as much as if my mother had
held me in her womb. A poem about adopted children points
out that a mother's adopted child was not carried in her
womb but carried in her heart. I know this is true in my
case. Many people believe that giving birth to a child makes
a woman a mother. I disagree. Motherhood comes from
patience, love, and a myriad of other God-given emotions.

Adoption reminds me of the way Jesus was brought to
this earth. He was raised by parents chosen for Him by God.
I believe Jesus handpicked my mother and father to raise
and nurture me so I can serve God on earth much as Jesus
served Him. Psalm 139:16 states: "Thine eyes did see
my substance, yet being unperfect; and in thy book all my
members were written, which in continuance were fash-
ioned, when as yet there was none of them." God created

everything in this world. He chose to form me outside my mother's womb, then gave me to my parents.

My heart breaks when I see children who are troubled because they are adopted. . . . The questions about my adoption never stopped as I grew up, but they did not bother me. My pride in adoption often surprised them.

I praise the Lord that I was not aborted. I wish I could tell every young, unwed mother who wants to abort her child how selfish and wrong that is. God chooses whether to make life or take it away. No one else should make that choice. I believe that premarital sex is in direct opposition to what Jesus tells us in the Bible, but if a girl does become pregnant, I am unquestionably convinced it is her responsibility to carry that baby until birth.

Instead of aborting her unwanted child, what a wonderful gift a young girl could give to a couple by allowing them to love the child and nurture it in a Christian home. As the Bible says, our parents have us for only a short while. We do not belong to them; we belong to Jesus. We are His children because He loves us more than anyone else does. So we can have faith that no matter how He arranges our "living accommodations" here on earth, He loves us and "works all things together for our good."

He knows the number of hairs on our heads. He gave His life on the cross for you and me. At the end of time, He will bring His adopted children, those who have turned from sin to Him in saving faith, home to heaven.

Adapted from the *Fundamentalist Journal,* May 1989

9

"Whose Name Is on the Sign?"

As I see it, the greatest problem confronting today's youth is the lack of strong leadership in the home. Without this essential, God-ordained leadership, there is little protection against outside evils.

Every home needs a man who is willing to lead. I have yet to encounter a young person in trouble whose difficulty could not be traced directly to the lack of a strong father image in the home. Either the father was absent from the home, or he had lost his position as family leader by some improper action or actions that resulted in his becoming dysfunctional.

Today our liberal society seems bent on undermining the basic concept of marriage, advancing unbiblical feminist viewpoints, and ridiculing male authority. Such traditions will erode the effective father image. Take, for example, the numerous situation comedies on television where Father is the family idiot; look at the commercials, where Father is often the joke of the household; notice the cartoons, comic strips, books, and movies in which Father is depicted as the bungling mismanager.

It's all too easy for Dad to slip into the mold that society has shaped for him and abandon his responsibilities. The result of that attitude is increasingly evident in our juvenile courts. Without adequate leadership, our children have lost a vital feeling of security.

If a young man has no leadership in his parents' home, he is neither going to respond to authority anywhere else nor become a good leader in his own home or work, and certainly it will be difficult for him to submit to God's will.

If a young woman does not have a worthy father with whom to relate, she probably won't become a good wife or mother.

You don't have to take my word for it. Psychiatrists, psychologists, and family counselors have statistics to prove the need for a guiding father image in order to have a happy life.

In most cases, the only person who can provide a healthy father image in the home is the father. However, the father who tries to give his family every material blessing is not necessarily a good father, particularly if he withholds leadership and love.

A good father is a man who constantly tries to lead his family in the right direction. He says what he means and means what he says. We all make mistakes, but this is no excuse to quit. I'm glad my father didn't. I finally woke up to the fact that he was guiding me in the best way he knew, and I didn't know it all.

I've made plenty of my own mistakes. Years ago, when our daughter, Paula, was in elementary school, I was watching television, and she came up and said, "Daddy, see if I still fit." She wanted to see if I could still hold her on my lap like a baby. I nearly cried when I picked her up because her feet almost touched the floor. Where had the time gone? Why hadn't I done more with her, taken her places, spent more time with her?

I felt guilty for the time I had to be away from home lifting weights to make money for the Home, but I realized I had made the only decision I could, for in so doing I also shared the Good News of Christ. Yet I believe I still managed to spend more quality time with Paula than many dads do with their children.

The only way a man can lead his family in the right direction is by always seeking the divine guidance of God's Holy Spirit. A man can't do it alone.

Everyone likes to be a boss. At the Youth Home, I'm the boss. My name is on the sign out front. That has become somewhat of a joke at the Home, but it is no less true. Occasionally, I have to pull rank, and that's when I use the line, "Whose name is on the sign?" A new staff member may come to me with what he thinks is an ingenious solution to a chronic problem at the Home. Unfortunately, too often the solution is one I tried in previous years that proved ineffective.

I may tell myself that times have changed and the solution might work now. I may let the fellow worker find out for himself that his idea is wrong, or I may just give him a flat *no.*

When I do that, I'm sometimes met with a zealous, idealistic, "Why?"

"Have you seen the sign at the front of the house?"

"Yes, sir."

"And what does it say?"

"Paul Anderson Youth Home."

"Paul Anderson?"

"Yes, sir."

"That's my name."

"Yes, sir."

"My name is on the sign, and I say no."

"Yes, sir."

Someone has to make the final decisions. They are not always easy decisions. To some, being the boss may look desirable. I enjoy being the boss, but it's not always easy. When we're having fun, and when I want something my way, I ask, "Whose name is on the sign?" When things are tough and there are certain unpleasant responsibilities I must undertake simply because I am the boss, then I must ask myself, "Whose name is on the sign?" There's only one answer, and it keeps me going.

The boys have picked up on that question. When my wife and I have a disagreement, one of the boys may ask Glenda, "Whose name is on the sign?"

Even my daughter used to get in on the act before she was married. Once when Glenda and I were mildly disagreeing over something, Paula interrupted. "Mama," she said, "Daddy's name is on the sign."

One Sunday I arrived home during midafternoon after lifting and speaking at two services in a church several miles from Vidalia. As I pulled in the driveway, I was worried that something terrible might have happened. The place was surrounded by cars.

When I got in the house, I knew that nothing could be too seriously wrong. Glenda was smiling. She had invited our entire church congregation to the Home for a picnic. That was fine with me, but I was dog tired after a hard morning. I asked her to give my regards to our guests and told her I was heading for bed.

"Oh, no," she said. "I want you to help the boys get the horseshoe pits as well as the badminton and volleyball nets ready for our guests, and you also need to make everyone feel welcome."

I turned slowly, irritated. "Now, Glenda," I said, "I'm tired and I'm going to bed."

"You can't," she said. "Your name is on the sign."

So, no one has doubts as to who is in charge at the Paul Anderson Youth Home—not even Paul Anderson.

One Friday I arrived in Atlanta on a jet after speaking four or five times that day and then hopping planes. I drove from Atlanta to Vidalia, wondering all the way how I could somehow crawl into bed earlier than plans for the evening would allow.

I had cleared my schedule for the evening as I so often did during football season. Since several of our boys played football, I felt I should attend the games as any responsible father should.

I had almost justified not going and kept driving slower and slower, hoping the staff would already have left for the game by the time I arrived home. The game was another one hundred miles in the other direction, and I was simply too tired.

When I arrived, however, I was shocked and a bit disappointed to see that they had waited for me, and they had saved a special spot for me in the car: behind the steering wheel. I was glad when we got to the game, of course, realizing I had done the right thing, despite my fatigue. We were a little late, but I saw the play when one of our boys was hurt.

This family member collapsed on the field; I didn't think too much of it at first. I figured maybe he had the wind knocked out of him. When a doctor joined the coach on the field, I hurried down to see what was wrong.

"We need to get him to Macon immediately," the doctor said. "He is paralyzed, and it could be a brain injury."

Later in Macon, some sixty miles away, a neurosurgeon operated to check for a blood clot on the brain. After four hours of surgery, he reported that the boy had a chance to live. When I pressured him, he said the odds were fifty-fifty. My staff and I began to pray; then I gave them instructions for what needed to be done around the Home the next day.

"Aren't you going to be there?" one of them asked.

"No," I said. "I am staying in intensive care with our boy."

They were surprised and protested, "You've gone too long without sleep."

"That's all right," I said. "I'll stay."

Each staff member volunteered to stay, but I still declined. "I will stay because my name is on the sign."

God not only gave me the strength to stay with my boy all that night but He also strengthened him. Four days after surgery the neurosurgeon announced, "I can't understand it, but the young man has completely recovered. I see no reason why in a few more weeks he can't begin living a completely normal life again."

Only a week after the injury he was back in school.

God is good! My name is on the sign, but our heavenly Father is truly in charge of the Paul Anderson Youth Home.

10
Uplifting Speaker

One day when I was on the road much of the time, I began to take stock of just what it was I talked about so much to thousands of young people each year. First, I talked about Jesus Christ, of course, but I also had a great deal to say about physical fitness, patriotism, and the free-enterprise system. I began preaching my free-enterprise message after my first Russian trip in the early 1950s.

Through the years, I became concerned that the free-enterprise system was in danger. Polls showed that over 40 percent of high schoolers interviewed did not believe in businesses making a profit. A Harvard survey found that half the schoolchildren over ten who were questioned said they did not believe men who run large companies are honest. Another study revealed that the majority of college students were against a free market, and another indicated public confidence in business leadership had dropped from 57 percent to 20 percent.

I decided that concerned citizens needed to speak up for free enterprise before it died from a lack of understanding. In no way did I want to mix my preaching with my patriotic concern, but after all, our country was founded on Christian principles.

To overcome the many reasons for the low national image of

the capitalistic system, some friends and I started a nonprofit organization called Save American Free Enterprise, dedicated to educating future citizens and leaders concerning the challenges and fascinations of free enterprise. Often I was able to speak in many places for SAFE, whereas I might not have been given such an opportunity without that cause.

In 1967, with the help of a police escort, I spoke in eleven high schools and a junior high in one day in Charlottesville, Virginia; this was in addition to breakfast and dinner appearances. It could be a record; however, I usually spoke two or three times each day. Whenever I agreed to speak, I sent ahead a packet containing an assortment of photos for promotion, a blueprint for the table I used for my final feat, and a list of the weights I would need. The feats of strength were simply to gain attention. My purpose in any engagement was to reach the audience with a message. I had a problem in that I had three basic messages to convey, but I generally worked them all in.

First, of course, wherever possible I wanted to share my faith in Christ. If this was not communicated, all else was pretty meaningless. Second, I had my message on saving American free enterprise. Third, I wanted to let many, many people know about our Youth Home ministry.

I primarily spoke in churches, schools, colleges, and penal institutions, and at times to civic clubs, business and industry groups, and various others. In churches I stayed strictly with my Christian message. I don't like the emphasis on social work that has crept into our churches, especially the way it has affected what we hear from the pulpit. Obviously, I am not against social work, and I am convinced that our responsibilities are clearly stated by Christ in the New Testament, but the men in the pulpit, in my opinion, should project Christ.

If Christ is instilled in the hearts of the congregation, the social obligations will be met. A person whose life is changed and who is guided by the Holy Spirit will be concerned about his neighbor. Because of this, in my church appearances I preached Christ from the pulpit and encouraged pastors to do the same.

My lifting feats usually went over well in churches. A good speaker has to be entertaining, so I did a variety of lifts and kept my speaking entertaining as well. It was essential, considering the competition. People would just as soon have been at home watching what the television networks had cooked up for them with hundreds of thousands of dollars. When a pastor or weight-lifter tries to keep attention, his work is cut out for him.

Early in my career, I refrained from lifting in church sanctuaries, concerned that it might be in bad taste. Eventually I began including some minor feats of strength during these engagements, not because I was anxious to do so but because it was requested of me. Before long, my lifting in church became standard operating procedure, and I have seldom been criticized for it.

There was a pastor on the east coast in those years who criticized anyone and anything not agreeing with his methodology, so it didn't surprise me when he said, "I heard about your being in so-and-so's church and lifting weights right in the sanctuary, with all those young people playing that weird music."

The weird music to which he was referring was some beautiful guitar and banjo renditions of old hymns, a performance that had been rehearsed for months and was nothing like rock or jazz. It was more like Southern country style, and many were blessed by it.

"That pastor is always seeking the sensational," the east coast reverend concluded.

"I don't suppose you would go for anything sensational in your church," I said, having sensed a coldness among his people.

"That's for sure," he said.

"You know," I responded, "I read in the Bible about God coming to earth as a man, walking on water, making the lame walk and the blind see, healing the sick as well as raising the dead. He also allowed men to take His earthly life, sacrificing Himself for our sins, and then He was raised from the dead!" I began getting a bit louder as I preached to the preacher.

"The most sensational event in the universe is recorded in your Bible, and this church should be projecting it," I continued. "I don't believe you're doing that." I guess I lost a friend, but perhaps I opened his eyes a bit to the fact that, even if he couldn't justify certain types of music or athletic performances in his sanctuary, at least he should have become a little more enthusiastic about the content of Scripture so his people could smile a little more.

When I lifted in a church service, I prefaced my lifting (which preceded my actual speaking message) with a few remarks to explain my thoughts on exhibiting my gift. "You may have noticed," I began, "that I kept quiet when you all were singing the hymns. That's because I can't sing a note.

"Singing is not one of my talents, even though I enjoy hearing good singing and especially a beautiful voice. I personally cannot participate. I know it is particularly pleasing for all of us to hear someone praising God through singing, but my gift is a little bit different. I offer it to you here today to the glory of God, not as a show or a circus act or in any poor taste, but as a demonstration of the talent God has given me. I will attempt some feats in a respectable manner for His glory."

That generally eliminated criticism.

Many people wonder why I made a point of speaking so much in prisons. They knew that while I was interested in sharing Christ, I also needed to raise money for the Youth Home, and prisons are not places to raise money. I guess the main reason I leaned toward this ministry was the respect I received from the inmates, which led me to believe that my message was effective.

I found it a challenge to work with prisoners. A man who is being punished for breaking the law and who is of at least average intelligence is usually a highly motivated man who has taken the wrong path in life. He is often both aggressive and defensive and is one of the hardest to relate to. You really have to earn the right to be heard by a convict because he is especially suspicious of Christian speakers.

In my prison ministry, it took my entire lifting performance to try to break down the barriers and show the men I did not have a holier-than-thou attitude. I wanted them to begin thinking, *If I had been able to live with a man in a Youth Home like his, I would not have wound up in prison.* I wanted them to see that I cared and respected them for their motivation, if for nothing else. I wound up corresponding with many prisoners, and many became interested in weightlifting and in knowing Christ personally.

It was said that I held the record for annually speaking to more high schoolers than anyone else in the country, though high schools were not my main audiences. Officials often asked me to speak at high schools when they heard I was in town. On the whole, high schoolers are a tough audience. When I was in high school, I thought I had all the answers. I told high schoolers that when I was a teenager I was convinced I was adopted because I couldn't believe such a smart guy could have such stupid parents. Of course, I added, as did Mark Twain in a similar statement, I was amazed at how much smarter my parents became as I grew older.

One of the major points I wanted young people to realize was that they could do just about anything they wanted to do. The technology was available to them. The education and facilities were available. The only necessary requirements, I emphasized, were the drive, the determination, and the winning attitude. They could do as much or as little as they wanted.

Young people can fool their teachers, coaches, pastors, and parents, but they can never fool themselves or God. A person will not be honest with himself until he is honest with God. I couldn't tell them that immorality is not fun, exciting, or appealing, but I did remind them that no society has ever lasted a full generation after the moral structure has collapsed.

During those years of speaking in public schools, I had to be the judge of when and where to talk about my faith. There were enough independent crusaders who had contributed to the closing of high school assemblies to the Gospel. By overstepping their bounds, they could get away with what they considered a bold, powerful witness, but they also ruined any future outreach by other Christians. In more than one town, I was warned not to do what "that guy did who was here a couple of months ago."

However, experience showed me there was a way to work a clear testimony into a program without offending. If the message was a personal testimony and if no other groups were discriminated against, there was never a problem. No one ever hassled me about what I shared because I picked my spots carefully and was sensitive, though very direct. Giving an invitation or asking for commitments was out. However, I had no limitations in colleges, for I was usually invited to speak in chapel services, and college atmospheres were much freer.

Regardless of where I went, though, I tried to protect those who would follow me the next time. The longer the door stayed open to the Gospel, the more opportunities we all had to share Christ.

As I look back, I am thankful that nothing really embarrassing happened to me onstage. Of course, I came prepared. For instance, I never lifted a weight I could not handle. While what I lifted may have been three times what anyone in the audience could handle, it was generally just half my capacity. I also came prepared for clothing repairs.

That's right. I carried a needle and thread. Handling weights and performing other lifting feats well within my capacity ensured that I wouldn't be injured or embarrassed by not being able to successfully perform. However, with what my body had to go through in order for me to lift a dumbbell or a table loaded with men, my clothes were susceptible to embarrassing tears, especially before the age of double knits.

At a church banquet in Richmond, Virginia, I was doing my usual three-event exhibition. I one-handed a 250-pound dumbbell over my head from the floor. Then I wrapped the head of a twentypenny nail with cloth (to protect my palm) and drove it through two one-inch pine boards with my bare hand. Then came the real show.

I asked eight athletes who weighed about two hundred pounds each to sit on a specially designed table. When I knelt beneath it to lift it, my pants split in the back. Besides me, only the guys on the table were aware of it, and I heard them snickering. After I completed the lift and sat down, I could see them spreading the word throughout the crowd. While the pastor said a few words, I ducked into a little room and whipped a needle and thread from my wallet. I did a quick repair job and returned to the head table in time to individually greet the audience.

After saying hi or getting an autograph, the young people walked behind me to observe my ripped pants, but they were no longer torn. The athletes who thought they were going to make a fool of me wound up looking ridiculous. Happily, I had been prepared.

I enjoyed surprising audiences. It was no surprise to them that I could accomplish feats of strength, but people were generally shocked at my flexibility. This flexibility should lay to rest the ridiculous myths about weightlifters. To amplify this point, I often told crowds that I was too muscle-bound to scratch my back or rub my head, and all the while I would be scratching my back or rubbing my head.

During some of the awards banquets at which I was invited to speak, I usually was featured after all the trophies and other acknowledgments had been presented. By the time I was on the program, I had eaten supper and sat for nearly two hours. On my way to speak or perform, I would stop and put my foot on the table to loosen up. People were always amazed that I could do such a balletlike move. If there was room, and I was in the mood, I sometimes really surprised them with a flat-footed leap from the floor to the table in one bound (this depended on the strength of the table, of course). I could also skip rope fast and long. People remembered those shows of flexibility longer than the feats of strength or my talk.

I have an idea it was a surprise for the average audience that I had anything intelligent to say. They figured a professional athlete, especially a weightlifter, was just a one-dimensional man who knew nothing outside his sport. Sometimes I would let them keep thinking I was an ignoramus during the first five minutes of my speech when I shared a few funny stories. Often ''feeler'' lines were funnier than the jokes themselves. Example: "I pulled up to the motel and went in. Actually, I got out of the car first. Once I went in without unfastening my seat belt and realized I was dragging the car behind me."

That's all right for a joke, but there were people who would ask me later if that story were really true. They were the same types who asked me if I could straighten out a horseshoe or lift up their car. I could, but I wouldn't. I wanted to share two or three demonstrations that proved I was by far the strongest man in the world, and then I wanted to make my point that even I, the World's Strongest Man, could not successfully live a day without Jesus Christ. I did not want to be a freak or a sideshow.

As I said, the free-enterprise system had become more and more of an issue to me, so I spoke on it often. Sometimes it would provide me an opportunity to speak at schools where I might not otherwise have been invited, and of course, I was always able to work in at least a bit of a witness in those situations, though I didn't want to betray any official.

Once, after a demonstration and talk to a large group of junior high and high schoolers, I was signing autographs for the students. After about fifteen minutes, I realized that one of the boys had been through the line at least once before and maybe twice. I kept watch on him out of the corner of my eye. Sure enough, he got back in line and came through for another autograph.

I grabbed him by the shoulder. "What are you doing, son?" I asked, loud enough for others to hear.

"Oh, I believe what you said about free enterprise, Mr. Anderson," he remarked.

"What do you mean?"

"I'm selling your autographs."

What could I say?

To this day, I can usually tell by the look in a person's eye that he is going to say or do something cute. You would be surprised at the number of people who think they are making statements that are original. It must be the same for towering basketball players who are constantly asked, "How's the weather up there?"

When I weighed well over three hundred pounds, whenever anyone made a comment such as, "I'll bet your wife has trouble keeping enough food in the house," I would react dramatically.

"Congratulations," I would shout, "you're the one-millionth person who has said that to me, and I decided I would punch the millionth guy in the nose!"

Another favorite pastime of people at banquets was to gather around with cameras while I was eating. In my prime, I didn't eat much for a man of my size because I primarily lived on protein supplements. Consequently, I didn't want pictures taken showing me shoveling in the food. When I saw a camera pointed my way, I would sip my water or just poke at my food until the person relaxed. Then I would quickly take a bite before the camera bug could shoot. It was a challenge but not always fun. People needed to realize how they would feel if they were in my position.

High school students didn't know how to take me at first. They tried to figure out if I was an egotist, maniac, or some type of clown. Before I drove the twentypenny nail through the boards with my hand, I would tell the young people I could pile several boards high and break them with my hand "because I know karate, judo, jujitsu, and lots of other Japanese words," just to see how sharp they were.

When I became serious, they generally responded well. I would tell them I was there to entertain and inform, and I had no intention of talking down to them. I would say that they were not children; they were young adults. I also told them I would not use the word *kids* in referring to them. I explained that I wasn't going to attempt to capture their attention by using teenage slang expressions of the day. I made sure my audiences understood I was of another generation, and I was approaching them in a leadership capacity.

"What I will do is talk to you as adults," I bellowed. "I may shock you; I may surprise you. I won't apologize to you for my generation."

Then I would usually try some humor. Most high schoolers wouldn't laugh, even if they thought something was funny. If they laughed, they would sometimes feel as though they were capitulating too soon. Sometimes the students would groan or give a horselaugh. If necessary, I pointed out unruly students early and told them I expected to be the only one talking unless someone wanted to come up and challenge me for the floor. They usually laughed, not knowing exactly how to take me. Rather than telling jokes, I would try to stay with true, funny experiences or throwaway lines.

There were times when the straight truth got me into trouble as well. At one school I had two assemblies scheduled. During the first I said, as a bit of introduction to my message, "What I say here is not going to make any difference to you, young man, if you have already decided to risk your life holding up a supermarket to support your drug habit, or to you, young lady, if you have previously determined to sell your body on the street corner to the highest bidder for the same purpose. . . ."

Between assemblies an official asked me not to make this particular point in the second session. "We have some prostitutes in our school, and we wouldn't want to offend them," he said. I didn't openly respond to this statement but gave a silent Charlie Brown "Good grief."

One time someone asked me to speak at a college but to water down what I was going to say "unless you are willing to take the verbal abuse you will receive for talking about patriotism, free enterprise, or Christianity." I was not afraid of verbal abuse. Nothing could really hurt truth. I spoke and had no trouble.

Thank You Letters

Thank you, Brother Paul, for your Christian influence on so many young people. Years ago, we brought our three young sons to see and hear you at the Knoxville performance, and through your influence our twin boys (who are now 28 years old) added weightlifting to their schedules. They are now Christian teachers and coaches who work with youngsters.

Mrs. Honey Faye Yates, Tennessee (1979)

Your stirring and entertaining presentation to us last Friday was certainly the highlight of our Dilworth Rotary year. Your stalwart defense of our free-enterprise system is truly a joy to hear. How I wish there were more Paul Andersons roaming this country conveying this message.

John D. Hicks, Duke Power Company, Charlotte, North Carolina (1979)

I would like to take this opportunity to tell you how much the administration, faculty, and student body appreciated your sharing a part of your day with us. As a result of your visit to the "Original" Putnam City High School, each one of us is a better person. Your comments were timely, appropriate, and meaningful. The Principal's Leadership Class also appreciated the time you spent and the opportunity to visit with you.

Robert F. Butler, Principal, Putnam City High School, Oklahoma City, Oklahoma (1979)

I've heard other Christian athletes bring their testimonies, but none that I've heard equal what you did in our church on Wednesday night. I really believe that some of the conversions among the young men we had that night were most, most significant. You are a wonderful ambassador for our Lord.

Adrian P. Rogers, Pastor, First Baptist Church, Merritt Island, Florida (1968)

Your display of strength has always impressed me and your message about Jesus brought new inspiration to my life. My children are great admirers of you and would really appreciate a picture. Last night as I watched you I couldn't help but feel that we needed you on the moon. Why, you could have pulled that deep core out with one hand. Of course, the suit engineers would have a real challenge.

James B. Irwin, Colonel, USAF, NASA Astronaut (1972)

Your presence with us was a real delight and an inspiration. The midshipmen, as always, were challenged by your words and awed by your strength. We are always grateful to you and thankful to God, who is using Paul Anderson in a magnificent way.

Carroll Starling, Chaplain, United States Naval Academy (1973)

11
My Philosophy

In my heyday, I was miserable without a challenge. I could never stand having nothing to do. When there was nothing to work on or hammer out, I would create something. I enjoyed seeing how much I could do in a short time; I wanted to see how far I could drive or fly in a day or a week. I pushed myself to see how far a few hours of sleep would take me; if I had time to sleep as much as I really needed to, I was afraid my mind would stop working.

I do not recommend anyone pushing himself past a healthy limit, but running at full steam has always been my pattern, and I can't function any other way. I once asked a farmer if he had difficulty getting up at half-past four every morning. "It isn't hard when you're one hundred thousand dollars in debt!" he shot back. It's all a matter of motivation.

I knew how much money I needed to keep the Paul Anderson Youth Home open, as well as the fact that God wanted me to share the news of His love with as many people as possible, and I also wanted to advocate our American free-enterprise system that gives individuals freedom to succeed. That was my motivation.

Our boys at the Home were not totally aware of my schedule,

116

but they had a pretty good idea I was working overtime to make it possible for them to be with us. I wasn't too concerned about whether or not they appreciated what I was doing. I tell anyone who wants to get into this business that he cannot expect much gratitude from teenagers. I'm not putting down these wonderful, mysterious young people; I love having them around and being responsible for those that come under our care. However, I remember what I was like as a teenager, and it's a fact that many of these young people will not be thankful for what an adult does for them until later, when they can look back a few years.

Can manners be instilled in teens? Yes, though it may not be an easy task. As I stated earlier, we teach our boys to say "yes, sir" and "no, sir" (or "ma'am") and to say "thank you," but these won't become genuine expressions of respect and appreciation until later. Most young men just aren't made that way. Of course, those who are exceptions are a joy to have around, but we don't let their presence hinder our relationship with the others. The times I have difficulty with boys who do not seem grateful for our ministry to them is when they shirk their designated responsibilities. Then:

"You ate today, didn't you?"

"Yes, sir."

"If those of us responsible for raising funds don't do our jobs, then you won't eat. If you don't do yours, our property will not look presentable because of trash, litter, and unmowed grass. We have our jobs, and you have yours; we must all accept our responsibilities."

By letting them know they are part of the Paul Anderson Youth Home and there are certain responsibilities expected of them, we give them dignity. We want them to feel they must do their part to enable the Home to operate properly. Our aim is to teach our fellows that the world does not owe them a living.

During the Georgia pecan season, our boys gather pecans from our orchard, clean them, and package them to sell. The money derived enables our young men to buy Christmas presents for their families and other loved ones. We strive to teach our adolescents to be givers, not takers. During the Christmas season they make Christmas tree ornaments for many of our supporters, which gives our youths a chance to say thanks to those who do so much for them. This way the boys can feel they must not expect everyone to serve them.

Throughout the year, our fellows prepare and take food to needy families. They also visit nursing homes, where they sing, fellowship, and on occasion share their Christian testimonies. Our teenagers also assist local widows and elderly couples in moving furniture or doing other jobs that require muscle, which our students build plenty of in our bodybuilding program at the Home. Again, these activities provide opportunities for our family members to give of themselves to others.

The lesson I want our boys to learn is to discipline themselves to do those things they don't particularly enjoy. We must constantly remind ourselves—all of us—that we are simply paying our dues and that our work will pay off. Everything costs somebody something. I will argue with anyone who tells me that the word *free* is a valid description of any situation. The word should be stricken from our dictionaries. Anything someone gets free has been paid for by someone else. Take a Christian's salvation, for instance. It's a free gift, praise the Lord! I have already made it clear that I do not deserve salvation through any merits of my own. I couldn't have earned it even if it were to be earned. It was free to me. I simply received it. I was unworthy. Can you tell me that no one paid for it? My God gave His Son, and His Son gave His life. No, sir, salvation may have been free to me, but it wasn't free. Someone paid the ultimate price for it.

I am often asked how I have been able to do some of the things that appear so distasteful to others—and I'm not talking about the grueling traveling and speaking schedule I used to maintain. Someone in years past might have seen me drinking beef extract. "I don't see how you can do that," he'd say with a grimace. I didn't enjoy it. It just happened to be something I needed to do to maintain the body weight necessary to make me the strongest man in the world. There was no substitute for it. I am a slow eater. That means I didn't eat large quantities in my prime. To maintain my body weight, I needed tasteless gelatins, beef extracts, and solid proteins. It was no fun, but it was something I was willing to do.

Only the most dedicated athletes in the world can identify with what I am talking about when I mention the grueling, lonely hours of training. Runners have an idea of what it means to run and run and run with no one to cheer, no one even to watch. They are up before dawn and may run for hours, punishing their bodies so that when the big race comes they will be up to the test.

I have spent hours upon hours with nothing for company but the cold steel of hundreds of pounds of weights. No one was there to encourage me and push me on. No one was there to notice when I broke a personal world record by twenty pounds in a lift; no one would believe me until I did it in public. There was no glamour in the training room when I pushed my muscles to their limits, and I knew I should put in two more hours of murderous repetitions of an exercise I would never use. It was an exercise just to build one or two of the muscles I would use later in exhibition, and it would have been easy to talk myself out of it. What more was there to prove? Who would care? Why did I punish myself?

The reason is simple. When you want something, it will cost you. No gifts. No shortcuts. Sure, you can talk yourself out of it, but then what will you have? Only dreams of what might have been.

When that inner voice tried to convince me it no longer mattered, I just asked myself if I still wanted to be in great physical condition and regarded as the World's Strongest Man. When the muscles burned with pain and I felt the temptation to call it a day, I kept going.

What makes the difference? Determination. Will. Guts. Desire. Discipline. The extra mile, the one more hour of work, the constant battle against the mind; the realization that the man who works hardest and longest will be the man who excels.

No one really knew what I went through in the training room. The second-best lifters in the world had a vague idea, but the boys at the Home didn't need to know. I wasn't preparing them to be athletes, though many of them were and are today. I want my fellows to be productive. I want them to "never say die."

I want our family members to have the same attitude about their manners, actions, and social relationships that I have always had about my goals since beginning my weightlifting career. I earned the right to be regarded as history's strongest human. I do not have to defer to anybody, but I do. I call my elders "sir." I tell our young men that calling someone "sir" doesn't mean that you are inferior to him, but it means that you respect him. That makes it easier for them to call me "sir," though, as mentioned, I allow them to call me "Paul." I demand nothing more from them than I demand from myself.

I use the same mental attitude and procedure in my spiritual life. It's a constant battle to remain consistent and grow. In my prime I was physically stronger than anyone else and had a disciplined mind, yet I had a problem making time for personal Bible study and devotions. The difficulty with many active Christians is that they tell themselves they are doing the Lord's work anyway, so the personal time with Him can slip. Well, it can't! Time after time, I've seen an evangelist or an active layman spiritually run dry because he left God out of his personal life. It was something I really had to watch when I was traveling in connection with my lifting/speaking engagements. I had victory in the training room with my mental process. Satan couldn't beat me there, but he worked overtime on the little things that take less physical labor but more mental discipline.

I knew the only way I could resist temptation was by keeping in touch with the Lord through prayer and Bible study. When I didn't, my spiritual muscles grew lax. I needed someone to come along and encourage me and get me spiritually exercising again.

On one occasion I was particularly down; I wondered if it was all worth it. Daily I was working out—punishing myself—to remain the strongest man alive. I was traveling day and night and was away too long from my wife, daughter, and the boys. I wasn't seeing significant spiritual results through my speaking, and I was fighting that constant battle of trying to make time for prayer and personal Bible study.

Then God sent a man about thirty years of age who was understanding and had tremendous insight. He seemed to know what I was thinking. ''I know with your schedule and all that you do, you must get discouraged and wonder if your work is worthwhile,'' he said.

I just looked at him. I didn't want to admit he was right.

''I want to tell you that you visited our military base several years ago, and through your talk I received Christ,'' he said. ''I went on to seminary and now I'm pastoring a church.''

That was really a thrill. It kept me going.

Often I find that something I felt was minor had a major effect on someone's life. Each year I send out several hundred weight-lifting courses with manuals and photos. These have no expressly

Christian message in them, but I sign each course I send, "Your friend in Christ, Paul Anderson." More than once I have heard from someone who came to the Lord after investigating what I had meant by that.

In May 1967, I was invited to do a pregame performance at the minor league baseball park in Spartanburg, South Carolina. I turned down the request because I didn't merely want to be a sideshow. That isn't as ego-centered as it sounds. I felt I had something important to say, and people would more likely listen if I was the reason they came.

The president of the Spartanburg Phillies, Pat Williams, a twenty-six-year-old promoter, repeated his request and offered to let me say whatever I wanted. His team, a member of the Philadelphia Phillies system, was having a good year, and he wanted me to help him draw a big crowd. He was willing to pay a good honorarium and expenses and was so reassuring about letting me speak that I accepted.

I drove over two hundred miles from Vidalia to Spartanburg and "did my thing," including my lifting exhibition and giving a brief word of testimony concerning my encounter with Jesus. That night I signed a photograph in my usual manner for Pat Williams, and I found out later that he had thought it was pretty funny. In the presence of his secretary, he mocked what I had written, and she, being a Christian, told him he had better be extremely cautious in his choice of subjects for ridicule.

I also learned later that Pat had really been impressed by my message, particularly when I told the audience that I, the strongest man in the world, couldn't live a day without Jesus Christ. Pat continued to wonder about that, and other Christians made consistent impressions upon him until one day he went to a Christian friend and asked him for help in coming into a personal relationship with Christ.

Pat Williams became a dynamic, outspoken Christian and also the youngest general manager in the history of professional sports when in 1968, at twenty-eight, he took over the Chicago Bulls basketball team. He later became general manager of the Atlanta Hawks and from there accepted the same position with the Philadelphia 76ers. Pat left Philadelphia to organize the Orlando Magic, a new NBA team in Florida. He is active in the Fellowship of Christian Athletes, has written best-selling books with a Christ-centered message, and continues to speak to point people to Jesus.

Particularly thrilling to me is the way Pat and his wife, Jill, have opened their hearts and home by adopting eight children from overseas. Knowing that I had a little something to do with Pat's coming to the Savior has been of great encouragement to me.

But I am reminded in this instance that we simply must be faithful in communicating the Gospel. The Apostle Paul wrote:

> Who then is Paul, and who is Apollos, but ministers by whom ye believed, even as the Lord gave to every man? I have planted, Apollos watered; but God gave the increase. So then neither is he that planteth any thing, neither he that watereth; but God that giveth the increase.
>
> 1 Corinthians 3:5–7

A Show of Strength
By Pat Williams, General Manager,
Orlando Magic NBA Team

From the moment I got in on the promotional end of professional sports at the age of 24, I had big ambitions. By 1965 when I became general manager of the Philadelphia Phillies minor league baseball club in Spartanburg, South Carolina, I was determined to make a name for myself. I couldn't wait to try some ideas I hoped would pack Duncan Park, the ball field, with fans.

Part of the strategy for reaching that goal included lining up the strongest man in the world for a show of strength at one of our ball games in May 1967. His name was Paul Anderson. The former Olympic weightlifting champion appeared before a big crowd of 2,200 people. At five foot nine and almost 400 pounds, Paul was an impressive sight. His sleeveless pullover jersey exposed arms larger than most men's thighs; his chest was like a barrel.

After introducing Paul, I crouched in the Spartanburg dugout and watched with keen interest, knowing a piece of my success rode on Paul Anderson's act.

The first thing he did was take a nail in one hand and two one-inch planks in the other. He held the nail in his massive clenched fist, its point barely protruding. Then, raising his elbow as high as his ear, he slammed the nail down with such force that it penetrated the planks. The crowd gasped.

Next Paul walked over to two 85-pound dumbbells and lifted them with his little fingers. That feat finished, Paul pressed a 250-pound barbell over his head eight times, as if to condition himself for his finale.

And what a finale it was! Paul called our eight heaviest ball players onto the field. He had them sit on a wooden

Paul at Olympic Games in Melbourne, Australia, where he was a gold medalist, 1956.

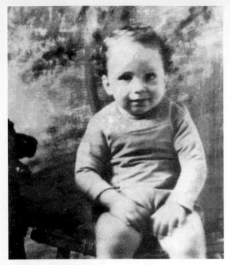

Paul at age two.

Toccoa High graduate, 1950.

Lifting steel wheels in home gym, 1954.

American weightlifting team in Moscow, Russia, 1955.

Meeting the Shah of Iran in Tehran, 1955.

Working out in Munich, Germany, 1955.

A smiling Paul exhibits the gold medal after his Olympic triumph.

A heavy clean before the jerk overhead.

A successful snatch.

Bench pressing more than six hundred pounds.

Exhibition at Black Mountain, North Carolina, Fellowship of Christian Athletes Conference, 1964.

The Andersons in front of the PAYH's Big House, 1964. (Kenneth Rogers, *Atlanta Journal & Constitution Magazine.*)

Paul sharing his testimony at a Billy Graham Crusade in London, England, 1966.

Senator Barry Goldwater presenting Paul with the Outstanding Young Man award, 1967.

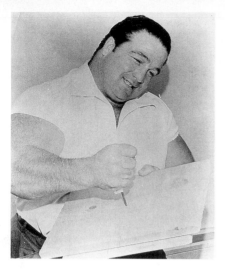

Above left: Paul driving a twentypenny nail through two inches of lumber with his hand.

Above right: One-arm dumbbell lift, Bradenton, Florida, 1969.

Right: Paul lifting a Pinto in front of the PAYH Big House.

Speaking at a youth rally in Macon, Georgia.

Paul with the women in his life — wife, Glenda, and daughter, Paula, 1972.

Grand Marshal of a parade in Perry, Georgia, 1973.

The climax of an appearance by Paul Anderson: lifting a tableful of men.

Paul with some of his boys, 1973.

Above: Speaking to inmates at Waupun, Wisconsin, prison in 1975.

Left: Paul, Glenda, and Paula on the patio behind the Big House, PAYH campus, 1976.

Above: May 25, 1983. Paul Anderson Day, Toccoa, Georgia. Dot Johnson, Paula, and Tom Landry. Sixteen-ton granite marker unveiled in front of Paul's birthplace.

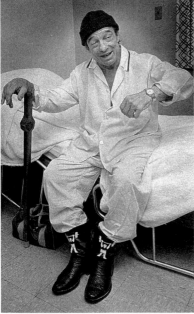

Left: At the University of Minnesota Hospital one week after kidney transplant, June 1983. (AP Wide World Photos.)

Paul talking with Governor and Mrs. Joe Frank Harris after he addressed the Governor's Prayer Breakfast in Atlanta, Georgia, 1984. (The *Atlanta Journal & Constitution* — staff photo by Dwight Ross, Jr.)

A quiet moment in the Big House chapel.

Paul, Glenda, and Paula at the Father of the Year Banquet in Atlanta, Georgia, where he was named Father of the Year — Humanitarian, 1984.

Paul with President George Bush in Washington, D.C., 1984.

Left: Glenda, Paula, and Paul on the campus of the Paul Anderson Youth Home.

Below: Glenda and members of the PAYH family, May 1988.

Left: Paul, Glenda, Paula, and Edward after the Anderson-Schaefer wedding, October 14, 1989.

Above: PAYH family in front of the Big House, dressed for the Anderson-Schaefer wedding.

Right: Glenda and Paul with Gerry Achenbach (standing, left), third incorporator of the PAYH, board of trustees chairman emeritus, past founder and president of Piggly Wiggly Southern; Truett Cathy (standing, right), first contributor to the PAYH, PAYH board of trustees, founder and president of Chick-fil-A; John Shea (seated), PAYH board of trustees chairman, president of Shea and Company.

platform we'd built in advance to his specifications. Each player weighed over 200 pounds, so I knew the total weight had to be nearly a ton.

Paul positioned his shoulders under the platform and began to try to lift it. Every muscle in that enormous body quivered. Then with a tremendous surge that made him look as if he were going to explode, Paul raised the platform. The crowd went wild.

I was feeling great as I left the dugout. Obviously the fans had been thrilled. Paul's act was a big hit. But what was happening now? Paul was making some sort of a speech. He had ignored the field mike and was addressing the crowd in a voice as powerful as his body.

"I've lifted more weight than anyone in the history of mankind," he roared. "I once lifted over 6,000 pounds in a back lift. I've been declared a wonder of nature from the United States to the Soviet Union." I was astonished at his lack of modesty as his voice reverberated through the ballpark.

"I've been written up in *Ripley's Believe It or Not*. I've stood on the center platform at the Olympic Games. They call me the strongest man in the world."

He paused. I hoped he was finished because this egotistical bombast was ruining his act. I was afraid this guy was about to do me more harm than good. But he continued, and what he said next was even more astounding.

"I want you to know, ladies and gentlemen, that all of these things are secondary in my life. I, Paul Anderson, the strongest man on the face of the earth, can't get through a minute of the day without Jesus Christ. The greatest thing in my life is being a Christian. If I can't make it without Christ, how about the rest of you?"

It wasn't the first time I'd heard Jesus Christ's name in a

ballpark. Profanity is pretty common among players and fans alike. But here was a gifted performer and an Olympic champion using Christ's name in a totally different way. It triggered something inside me, but I wasn't sure what.

After receiving one of the warmest ovations I'd ever heard in Duncan Park, Paul came to my office to autograph a picture of himself. On it he wrote, "To Pat, Your Friend in Christ, Paul Anderson." I didn't know how to handle that comment, but I framed the picture and hung it in my office.

Thanks to Paul Anderson and some of the other promotional acts that season, I was named the *Sporting News* Outstanding Class A Minor League Baseball Executive of 1967. But the award I'd coveted turned out to be only another temporary high for an empty young man.

Fortunately, the seed planted by Paul Anderson took root. An avid reader of sports books, I began to read about Christian athletes. Finally, in February 1968, I received Jesus Christ into my life, and He has kept me filled with joy, peace, and excitement—all at the same time—ever since.

Because Paul Anderson, like the Apostle Paul, was willing to testify for Christ, I learned that the strongest man in the world can't get through a day without Jesus. I've also learned Pat Williams can't either. I wouldn't have it any other way.

12
Years of Decision

I have often been asked if my autobiography published in 1975—the chapters that precede this one—truly represented my life story. With a look of surprise, my answer has always been, "No, not really, for if it were my *life* story, I would be dead!" My singular desire to win souls for the kingdom continues to be the same, even though my procedures have been altered because of my failing health. The years since 1975 have brought many additional wonderful and interesting experiences. I have also come face-to-face with new and even traumatic challenges—some so difficult that later in this new edition of my autobiography my wife, Glenda, will have to tell part of my story.

I believe that when a person attempts to relate his life story, the mind is prone to recall more painful situations than pleasant moments; unfortunately, the tranquil events do not seem to be as indelibly etched in the memory. As I look back, next to the bad things that happened in my life, the humorous incidents win second place. This is why you have read and will read more about the tragic and humorous experiences instead of the happy, rewarding ones.

My schedule on the road did not change a great deal during 1976. The engagements themselves stayed about the same as I journeyed to churches, banquets, prisons, high schools, and colleges.

I continued to do weightlifting performances, although more and more I began to think about phasing out my exhibitions. One reason was that I wanted to see if I could hold the attention of audiences without doing the demonstrations. Common sense also taught me that I could not go on forever lifting tremendous poundages, especially without warming up. Even without the age factor, I constantly faced the danger of slippery floors, unstable carpets, and other conditions not conducive to a good footing for lifting.

During the spring of 1976, I began to let up on some of the high school engagements because many principals warned me before going onstage that I could say nothing at all about the Lord or witness in any way. This completely defeated my purpose for being there, so I started checking these invitations before confirming the request for such assemblies. Merely presenting my cause and receiving negative responses from some of these frightened administrators of our public schools eliminated some of the school appearances. To compensate, I added more crusade-type programs and began choosing the ones where I would be the main speaker and not a special side attraction.

Countless organizations, including churches, started having week-long revivals or crusades with a different speaker each night. This is why I found myself, in April 1976, flying into National Airport in Washington, D.C., for an appearance I would long remember.

Actually, this was a great performance for a young man who rented local high school auditoriums and held crusades on Friday and Saturday nights. Otherwise he did an effective street ministry by witnessing to government officials and even to foreign individuals who had business in Washington. I admired his Christian fortitude and usually accepted his invitation when he requested that I appear at one of his rallies.

After my plane had landed and I went through the routine of getting my bags and renting a car, I became nauseated and light-headed as I rode the Perimeter Road counterclockwise around Washington. My first thought was that the shrimp-and-steak combination I ate on the plane had poisoned me. I also remembered that at the Youth Home we had been experiencing a "bug" that affected the body in this way, and I wondered if I was coming down with it.

It was all I could do to check into the motel, where a reservation had been made for me, and get to my assigned room before the evidence of my nausea began to manifest itself. In fact, I had to regurgitate about every fifteen minutes. At this point, it was about half-past three or four o'clock in the afternoon, and I knew if I didn't get some type of relief I could by no means do an evening program. I was too ill to stand before a crowd and speak, much less do my lifting feats. There was also the factor of dehydration entering the picture. I called my host and explained my predicament, but he passed it off with, "I'm sorry," and proceeded to tell me what time he would pick me up.

Perhaps if I had been in his shoes, I would have had the same attitude. He had advertised I was going to be there, and it would have put great pressure on him for me to be a no-show. I was determined to go to the rally, but I merely wanted to warn him about my condition. I asked him to bring along some Dramamine when he came to take me to the engagement, hoping this medication would curb my nausea.

By the time my host arrived at the motel, I had managed to get dressed as I continued to fill the plastic trash can. When I walked out to his car, I carried the freshly emptied trash can. The promoter had another man with him, so I suggested that he drive my rented car and allow me to sit on the passenger side. By doing this, I would have a way to return if I needed to leave early.

Our meeting place was a high school auditorium on the Maryland side of Washington. It was filling up rapidly as I looked at the crowd from behind the stage curtain and continued to use the trash can. I knew I would receive a certain flow of adrenaline when it was time for me to go on, which would help me face the obligation a little better. I also knew I could very possibly receive one of those sickness calls while I was in the middle of my message.

The preliminaries were over, and when I was introduced I told my friend who was promoting the program that he might have to come out anytime and take over. I left my trash can just inside the curtain so it would be handy.

On stage, I explained to the audience that I was suffering from what appeared to be a case of food poisoning and requested that they please bear with me and also pray I would be able to do God's work that evening. I didn't like to start a program on this negative note, but I really felt things were not going to go smoothly.

My first feat was to drive a twentypenny nail through a board with my hand. I managed that without difficulty. Later in the program, I would lift eight or nine men seated on the table that had been built for me. I was indeed glad that the table was there on the stage, for not only did I place the board on it for the nail-driving feat but I also used it to steady myself several times that evening.

When I got into my message and began feeling a little better, I started to move about the stage. Taking several steps toward my audience to emphasize a point, I suddenly knew it was all over. I felt terribly unsteady, as though the stage were trembling beneath me. Each time I took a step I actually thought the platform was moving. A feeling of fear came over me because I knew this unsteadiness was getting worse, and I could crash to the floor.

Surely illness is going to come to us all, and although our minds can play many tricks on us and even make us ill through various degrees of suggestion, this time I had almost blown the evening by allowing an outside influence to make me completely give up on my delivery. You see, I was not getting worse at all. Without knowing it, I had stepped out onto a temporary portion of the stage that was on wheels and blended in perfectly with the permanent area. With my great body in motion, the platform trembled and rolled on its casters. Considering my physical condition, I just knew my time had come; fortunately, I stepped back a few feet and realized I had simply been standing on shaky ground!

After my message, I lifted the table, which held men whose weight totaled approximately fifteen hundred pounds; then I quickly slipped out the back door and returned to my motel. That night I drank liquids to overcome my dehydration and continued to take Dramamine. By morning I felt much better and more confident that the next exhibition, scheduled for that evening, would be a steadier experience.

Other than a rare illness, my greatest problem in my traveling days was lack of sleep. There was no way I could constantly travel and get a proper amount of rest. After I was out on a trip for a few days, this lack of sleep began to present itself more prominently, and I often resorted to catnaps while waiting for planes, as I flew, and even as I rode in taxicabs.

One time during the early summer of 1976, I had been traveling for about three days. On the third evening, I spoke at Estes Park, Colorado, for the Fellowship of Christian Athletes. I had many friends and acquaintances there, and after my message I stayed up late visiting with them. This bull session lasted much longer than I would have liked, but it was taking place in my room at the YMCA camp where the conference was being held, and I couldn't politely evict my friends. If I had been in someone else's quarters I could easily have said good night and excused myself, but I had to suffer it out until about 3:00 A.M.

My plane left Denver at 10:00 A.M., so I had to rise about half-past five and drive the two hours back to Denver during heavy rush-hour traffic and work my way across town to the airport. Needless to say, when I had turned in my rented car, checked my luggage, and gotten my seat selection straightened out, I used the next few minutes before flight time for a quick nap. I found a seat next to a busy corridor, close to where I would board my plane.

I was more tired than I had thought and immediately fell into a rather deep sleep. My head fell into a position that caused snoring, which evidently worked into a grand crescendo, for I jumped in the middle of a great snort and leaped to my feet. Just then a meek-looking, well-dressed gentleman wearing a homburg and carrying an umbrella and a briefcase was passing in front of me. For some reason a leaping, snorting 375-pounder scared the wits out of him. He let out a shriek and tossed his umbrella and briefcase into the air. I turned as nonchalantly as possible and hurriedly entered the gate to my now-boarding aircraft. Behind me, I heard a lot of talk and the sound of a crowd gathering around the distinguished little gentleman with a problem, but I never dared to look back.

In the summer of '76, after returning home from the FCA conference in Colorado, I checked my calendar and found it would actually be easier if I continued my summer schedule from the Dallas Home that was then under our direction instead of from our Youth Home in Georgia.

In 1972 we had expanded to Texas at the request of now-deceased Judge Russell of Dallas and several probation officers who had seen that our system worked. We never had ambitions of building additional homes. Our goal has always been to establish a model project of spiritual guidance, academic excellence, and physical fitness that hopefully would be adopted by private and public institutions throughout the nation. All of this is being done at the Paul Anderson Youth Home in Vidalia. The PAYH has helped individuals who desire to start homes. We gave five institutions our name for a period of time to add validity to their efforts, which also gave them the right to use our system of teaching. Others have received our program but did not choose to operate under our name. For example, we can point out homes in different parts of the country to which we gave our program and personal guidance, but they used the names of local persons or people whose names would be significant in their particular geographic region.

In Dallas I was only ten minutes from the airport and the Texas Home really needed more of my attention. So, feeling it would almost be a vacation, Glenda and I, with our nine-year-old daughter, Paula, headed for Dallas.

It was a real pleasure to have someone take me to the airport and pick me up, a contrast to my eight-hour Vidalia-Atlanta round-trip. Not only was the Dallas situation convenient but it also allowed me to spend much more time with my family. It was a joyous time, though I still had to be away a lot.

One afternoon when Paula and I were alone at the Texas campus, I learned a lesson concerning family relationships. It was a dude ranch setting, and the facilities had been there for many years. The walkways and patios, made of native stone, had rather rough surfaces. Paula was running across one of those patios and stumbled on a protruding stone. She took a bad fall, skinning her elbows and knees and temporarily losing her breath.

Paula and I had grown even closer to each other in the last few days. We had made the trip to Texas together, driving out because we needed our car in Dallas. Glenda had flown out several days later since she had to finish some work in Vidalia.

When Paula took her fall, she reverted back into a small child and rushed to my waiting arms. She was crying, and I picked her up and consoled her, telling her I would doctor her wounds with medicine I promised would not burn. I think I really felt the ultimate in fatherhood right then because ordinarily a child her age would run to her mother when she was injured. Not long after the fall Glenda returned from an errand, and when Paula saw her mother, she once again started weeping and began a detailed account of her terrible tumble. She then held her arms out to her mother and said, "Mommy, you weren't here when I fell, so I had to go to Daddy." Needless to say, this immediately destroyed my great bubble of fatherly pride!

I soon recovered from Paula's sending my fatherly spirits tumbling, and I was back on the road tending to my busy schedule. In early 1977, the American Academy of Achievement invited me to Orlando to receive an award. I had heard of the organization, but when the invitation arrived, I had little idea about the importance of the occasion. However, as additional materials were sent to me, I grew progressively more impressed by seeing who had been the previous recipients. They included heads of state, such prominent movie stars as John Wayne, and many giants in business and industry.

After Glenda, Paula, and I arrived in Florida, we had the

privilege of attending various parties connected with the presentation scheduled for the next evening. We met renowned newscaster-author Lowell Thomas, newsman John Chancellor, and war hero Lieutenant General James H. Doolittle. I also found out that the hero of the famed Entebbe rescue of the Israeli hostages, Brigadier General Dan Shomrom, was also to be honored. Others included entertainment personalities such as Stevie Wonder, research scientists who had made amazing contributions in artificial heart work and cancer research, prominent authors such as Alex Haley of *Roots* fame, and the great insurance magnate John McArthur. With so many "household names" and other prominent people on the list, I actually began to wonder, *What am I doing here?* Why was Paul Anderson, a weightlifting champion and youth worker, in this company?

The night of the dinner was even more impressive. Many past recipients were there, top names from *Who's Who* in various areas of life. There was much pomp and ceremony connected with this organization and its functions, and everything was done to perfection. Each person had a time limit for his or her response to receiving this coveted award. I wondered what I should say. As I mentioned before, I've never believed in a humble, clod-kicking response, but this would be the most impressive and influential group of people before whom I had ever had the opportunity to stand.

As always, my first thought returned to the main interest in my life, my Christian witness. I reflected on how wonderful it would be there, among some of the world's elite, to say something about belonging to the Lord Jesus Christ; then, as always, Satan's deception entered into the picture. "Paul," Satan seemed to whisper, "don't be a fool by taking advantage of this situation; you will make those around you uncomfortable!" Suddenly, I recalled that twenty-two years ago I had had an opportunity to speak of Christ in the Soviet Union, but because I was then only a pseudo-Christian I had had nothing to say. No, now I would not let another opportunity escape.

I was sitting next to a friendly, award-winning television and screen actor. As we talked, I realized I was going on first, since awards were to be presented in alphabetical order. I wondered what his attitude would be after I went up and received my medal, golden plate, and other gifts and spoke of my relationship with Jesus. Once again Satan tried to put doubts in my mind: "This famous movie star will think he is sitting next to a religious fanatic!" While these thoughts were speeding through my mind, I heard the master of ceremonies calling me forward. My going up before the hundreds of people gathered there was by no means a trying experience. Addressing people was my business, but deciding on just what was appropriate to say made me uneasy.

As I stepped to the front of the stage and was given the microphone for my two-minute remarks, the celebrities and stars no longer dazzled me; they were simply people who had done well in their own fields. Besides the fact that I had achieved much in my line of endeavor, I was also a child of the King of the Universe! This last fact alone lifted me above and beyond any human station. I proceeded to say a few words about my interest in our great American free-enterprise system and responded to some comments that had been made about our work with boys. I told the academy how much I appreciated this honor and that I would place the award among my most treasured accolades.

Then, in words as bold as I could muster, I said I wanted to speak briefly about the most wonderful event that ever took place in the universe and how it had led to the greatest experience in my life. In conclusion I said, "My greatest thrill is having the privilege to be a Christian and witness to others about Jesus Christ, my Lord.'' If this made me a fanatic, I did not care. As I turned to walk away, I heard a tremendous ovation from the audience. When I got back to my seat, the previously mentioned actor looked at me with tongue-in-cheek disgust and said, ''How do you expect me to follow something like that?''

As I was driving home from the Florida engagement, I thought of witnessing and how the opportunity presented itself so often in my life. I thanked God for giving me these chances, but suddenly I began to realize that, even though I was doing much preaching and talking about the Lord to audiences throughout the U.S. and on trips abroad, we were not doing a great deal of this at the Paul Anderson Youth Homes. Yes, we took the boys to church. We even had daily devotions, but otherwise they were not being taught God's Word the way they should have been.

The more I thought about this, the more I began to realize that during the short time—about a year—we had the privilege of working with our boys—primarily sixteen, seventeen, and eighteen years of age—we allowed them to be out of our care too much. They were going to public school for about seven hours a day—up to ten hours, with extracurricular activities. Somehow we needed a plan to instill Christian principles in them at the Home; we simply were not making enough of our opportunity. Now God was showing me the problem, so I asked Him for an answer.

As I continued to think and pray, I realized that many of our supporters would say we had been very successful in the operation of our ministry, so why should it change in any way? My answer to this was that times had changed and even our opportunity to work with the boys was shorter than before. The juvenile courts had begun to decrease their probation periods, which meant the young fellows stayed in our custody only about half as long as they had previously. Therefore, just to break even, we had to give them twice as much as we had in the past. To accomplish this, I felt we could no longer afford the time our teenagers were spending in public school. Their needs called for more specialization to accomplish our goals in the time frame in which we had to work.

I remembered what I had recently read concerning the ideas and philosophy of the world's richest man, J. Paul Getty. He had said that from time to time he felt the necessity to change his business methods. These operational procedures had to be modified to suit the times. He had gone on, however, to emphasize that ethics and moral obligations never change in the business world, but our methods must. Contemplating our problem and feeling that Almighty God was leading, and also thinking of the statement by Getty, I decided we should start our own school system at the Youth Homes.

When I returned home, I wrote up all of my suggestions concerning a new program for our work. My projection stated that the Vidalia Home would set the example for other homes then under our direction by starting its own school and using an accelerated program to meet our boys' needs right where they were academically, spiritually, physically, emotionally, and socially and bring them to the point where we felt they would be prepared to go out into the world and be solid citizens.

I was deeply disappointed that my proposals were not met with an enthusiastic reception from my board of trustees and other key people who were involved in our youth ministry. I was so carried away with the idea that I wanted everyone else to be just as excited. At our next board meeting, I explained this and the need for the program, and I could see some of our people reacting and could almost read their minds. I surmised they were thinking that, if my plans were approved, no longer would our boys be the stars on the local football field and provide us the welcome public relations boost we had been receiving. Others undoubtedly felt we would become isolated from the community by following this course and maybe even alienate many local residents.

Happily, I was fortunate enough to have an individual among these dedicated leaders openly share my enthusiasm. It was gratifying to see one of my newest and youngest board members, Truett Andrew, the wife of local attorney Charles Andrew, say she thought this was a grand idea and she would like to head the program. She taught at our county's private school and had the reputation of being the best teacher around. She was called a teacher's teacher, even though she was only in her early twenties.

My gratification from Truett's support immediately turned to uneasiness. I was afraid that the administrators of the private school where she taught and all the parents whose children attended there would certainly become alienated if I allowed her to terminate her position and start teaching at the Youth Home. Later I discussed this apprehension with Truett, and she assured me she would resign since it was completely her idea and I had not approached her at all. Because this was the absolute truth, I felt more comfortable with the idea.

The remaining members of my board began to see the advantages of an on-campus school as we started to put together our curriculum. Different, newer, and more pleasant ways were given to us to get messages across to young people. Our whole idea was to make learning a pleasure.

From the beginning of our school in Vidalia, God has blessed our efforts and enabled us to make it a successful venture. The school truly became a learning place, as it is to this day. We start the morning with Bible study and often spend several hours in God's Word. We find we can go right through our Bible study time and ease into other academic subjects in a smooth and interesting way. On many occasions, we have vocabulary lessons from our Bible study and discussions. This might lead us into grammar, and even as we study the Old Testament we document ancient history as well. When we pinpoint events in history that happened in the same time periods in which biblical events took place, the Bible study becomes more interesting because the boys know what else was going on in the world at the same time. Yes, it has all turned into a tremendous blessing. Why not—it was inspired and guided by Almighty God!

To further substantiate the success of our school system, I can give many examples of young men who have gone through three grades of high school in a one-year period. We sometimes even preregister fellows in college and teach them from the college textbooks they will have as freshmen. When they arrive on campus, they feel secure and are able to fit in and make good grades right away.

Having our own academic program has many side benefits other than just learning. Teenagers who have had drug problems are not tempted by the drugs that are available in almost all public schools. We have a greater influence during a twenty-four-hour period with our young fellows because we have them the entire time. We have spiced up the classes with visiting speakers who teach our boys practical skills such as opening bank accounts, buying and financing automobiles, purchasing insurance, and filing income tax forms. We even have a collection of menus from outstanding restaurants around the country, and we teach our family of boys how to order from these menus, to give them more confidence later in life. On occasion, we actually go to restaurants, take field trips, and visit businesses, industries, and places of historical interest.

I give the Lord full credit for leading Glenda and me into our work with boys, and I also thank Him for guiding us into the school program. As I encountered others who did not quite understand what I was planning to do with an on-campus school, I grew even more grateful for Glenda's confidence and dedication. From the start, she seemed to think my idea was very good. A man needs this type of support from his wife if he is going to forge ahead in the everyday world, much less undertake the kind of challenges we have been given.

13
Years of Change

The year 1978 found me turning forty-six years old, and even though I had been a physical culturist and exercise buff since college days, my schedule and the tremendous lifting I had done onstage without warming up were taking their toll. Besides this, I had to consider the injuries I had suffered, including the damage to my hip joints and lower back caused by the 1954 auto accident. It was rather comical to me when sportswriters said in their articles that I walked with the swaggering gait of a weightlifter. I don't know why they thought a weightlifter should walk any different from someone else! Actually, I walked with a swaggering gait because my entire body had been knocked out of line and damaged when that car hit the tree after sliding off the highway.

I was able to temporarily triumph over this physical damage because youth was on my side and I was in good physical condition. My injuries hurt, but I was able to overcome them and forge ahead. Even though the accident not only injured my hips and lower back but also broke several ribs, after a short time I had returned to lifting. My real problem was that I could never walk comfortably after the wreck.

I suppose personal pride always made me not want to face the fact that I was somewhat crippled; after all, I could run quite fast for my size. Only when I had to confess on occasion that I could not walk long distances, such as when I was in Russia, did I own up to my handicap. Growing older seemed to bring the hip problem to a more prominent light in my everyday activities. More and more my right hip gave me painful arguments when I walked long distances.

I remember well the first time I actually had to stop to ease the type of spasm that bothered me at times. It happened in 1978 in the Detroit airport terminal, where it seems you must sometimes walk miles to transfer from one plane to another. Although I felt discomfort caused by the hip-joint injury and suffered some pain when getting up, sitting down, or getting cold, I never quite experienced the spasmodic tightening and shooting pains that came over my right hip and leg on that particular spring day. There were benches along the corridor where I was walking, and though I felt it was giving in to my weakness, I just had to stop at one of these to rest for a moment.

I will never believe anything except that this rest period was God's will. I had just taken a seat when an airport janitorial employee came by tidying up the area. She appeared to be in her thirties and was attractive and well groomed. Ordinarily, I would not have noticed her as we met in that busy transportation interchange, but she was emptying the ashtray just in front of me. Due to my size I am usually noticed, and as she took a second glance, she said, "I believe I have seen you on one of the religious television programs." I was delighted that I apparently had found a sister in Christ with whom to visit for a few moments. I confirmed her assumption and asked about her particular church and spiritual life.

Because I am a very private person, I could never approach an individual about his or her spiritual well-being unless some door was opened for me by the Holy Spirit. In this case, I was not really questioning the woman's salvation but just making Christian conversation. She became evasive, and I found myself acting somewhat out of character by asking her if she were a Christian. She gave me the old stock answer, "I try to be." This gave me an opportunity to thoroughly witness to her concerning salvation through Jesus Christ; I am convinced that the Holy Spirit used our meeting in a grand and productive way.

Yes, I do believe my hip problem became accelerated just to stop me at that time and place so I could speak to this woman whom God had prepared for His message that day. If human infirmities are going to plague me in a manner that allows my witness to be used in a better way, I welcome them.

I knew what my situation would be before long if I did not get some help for my ailing hip. I realized that arthritis ran in my family, and this old injury would certainly be a real invitation for the crippling disease to enter and take over. I immediately consulted a doctor and began to feel much better after he prescribed aspirin and prednisone, an anti-inflammatory preparation that is a type of cortisone. I even experienced some freedom and mobility that I had no idea I had lost. Unfortunately, my relief was short-lived because I could not tolerate the side effects caused by prednisone, and aspirin for me is really bad news as well.

In May 1978, when I arrived in Vidalia after a trip to Washington, D.C., where I had been the speaker for the Senators Prayer Breakfast, I felt nauseated. The condition worsened and I began to regurgitate. I was shocked to find that my stomach was bleeding. I went to our local hospital and was admitted to intensive care to be constantly monitored to see if my blood pressure was holding or if the hemorrhaging was causing my body to grow weaker.

My doctor told me that eight out of ten such cases usually require no surgery and healing soon takes place with proper care. I was grateful to Almighty God that in a few days I was home and beginning to regain my strength. I followed a strict diet and went on a strenuous swimming and water-exercising program.

While in the hospital, I received several pints of blood but asked that no more than was absolutely necessary be given me. This was before blood could easily be checked for hepatitis, and I knew from my mother's bad experience the results of receiving contaminated blood. She had died in 1978 from cirrhosis of the liver contracted through blood infected with hepatitis she received during a 1975 operation.

I found that my endurance was quite limited. I took vitamin B_{12} shots and supplements to regain my hemoglobin count, which went back up in a matter of weeks.

I am sure there is no proper time to be ill, but fortunately I did not miss many engagements while I was having the stomach problems. I had some slack time set aside to do some work in the Vidalia office, so I was not letting anyone down. After I resumed my schedule, I felt fine and soon regained my endurance. Along with the swimming, I soon went back into my weightlifting, and my muscle tone returned rapidly because it had not suffered a great deal during the short illness.

As I continued my speaking schedule, I noticed that, on the occasions when I was not asked to perform my feats of strength, I really did much better addressing my audiences. Maybe I subconsciously felt obligated to put a little bit more behind my message because I did not have the weightlifting to enhance my program. Anyway, I began more and more to entertain the idea of giving up the lifting during my appearances. As mentioned earlier, there are many considerations to ponder in such a decision, but I really made up my mind one summer day as I appeared before inmates of Leavenworth Federal Prison near Kansas City, Kansas.

After my introductory film was shown on their regulation-size screen and received well, I went right into my routine. When it came time for the table lift, I asked for volunteers. It seemed they had been anticipating this moment, and eight of the largest men in the institution came up grinning and sat on the table. My first concern was whether or not the table could tolerate the strain. Despite the fact that the table swayed in the middle under an estimated combined weight of well over eighteen hundred pounds, I felt it was strong enough to hold and proceeded to position myself for the lift of all of this blubber and muscle. I pushed and the table rose from the floor in a most successful lift, as the audience cheered approval. In this perfect lift, with a poundage much heavier than usual, I must have had my feet closer together than normal because the table rose higher than in most cases. Then I observed the conditions about me: the floor was slippery; the table actually was not as well built as I had previously thought, and what's more, I had not warmed up. What a chance I had taken!

As I was being driven back to the airport, I thought of professional football players and other athletes who had continued to play the game too long and became ineffective because of their lack of speed, coordination, and strength, as well as their ability to take punishment. I was doing as well as ever and had been fortunate not to have received any serious injuries from the bad conditions under which I had to lift during engagements. Now was the time to stop!

You see, even though I successfully made that lift at the prison, I had tasted what many of these aging athletes suffer after their abilities start to ebb. I recalled a couple of occasions when my lifts were less than successful and my audiences misunderstood the situations. Both times I had considered phasing out my lifting during my speaking engagements.

Most of the time when I sent my table plan ahead, the table was built to the letter of instruction. On rare occasions, it was modified by well-meaning people who either thought they knew a better way to build it, misunderstood my plans, or even lacked the proper materials.

On one occasion, the table was not properly constructed and was far too flexible for a successful lift. When I got under it and pushed against the bottom with my back and completely straightened my legs, the legs of the table still remained on the floor because the table bent so much in the center. There was no possible way of lifting the structure when it was loaded to any respectable poundage. Somehow the audience felt I was not raising it because I could no longer perform the feat of strength. When the table legs failed to lift from the floor and I finally abandoned my efforts, I received scattered applause and some audible sighs and moans of sympathetic encouragement.

The other time this happened I received an identical response. It occurred because the table was about four feet too long, and there was no possible way to balance it. Each time this occurred I tried to explain the difficulty, but I doubt I sold my case very well. It gave me a sense of what it would be like one day if I really could not perform.

I certainly believed it was God's will that I discontinue my lifting exhibitions except on very special occasions so that I could still keep my dignity and respect. I knew some people would be disappointed, but my engagement requests were so numerous that I could be somewhat independent and choosy. As I saw later, my decision was a wise one.

In 1979, I spent time in Texas working with the Youth Homes. During this period I was increasingly plagued by kidney stones. I had been bothered by this ailment through the years, but now attacks occurred quite frequently. Anyone who has suffered these problems knows how painful kidney stone attacks are, and though I did not need to cancel any engagements, I certainly went through difficult periods.

As long as I was able, I continued working with an organization involved in promoting programs for high school students to acquaint them with basic American values. Years earlier I had realized that our young people were more sophisticated and better educated than they had ever been in the history of our country. So many of them were patriotic, God-fearing young adults, searching for good leadership and respectful examples to follow. Responding to this need, I saw my work evolving into another type of ministry.

I began to feel that my work in Vidalia dealt with not only young adults but with their parents as well. This gave me an opportunity to help families fortify their lives and strengthen their households. I added a family seminar to my regular programs and used this on various occasions, ranging from two consecutive night meetings to Sunday-morning services. These were conducted in churches or were church sponsored in other facilities. I gained much satisfaction from these efforts.

One of the greatest problems I faced in carrying out these seminars was that, if church members and other interested parties realized it was a program to give families guidance and direction, pride kept many away. They believed people would think they had problems in their families, not realizing that even the best of our homes can certainly stand a little spiritual uplifting and moral strengthening.

During 1980, I also found myself driving much more. For years I had primarily flown to my engagements, either commercially or by private plane. We had owned two planes, and I had sold our last one because of the tremendous rise in the price of gasoline. The cost of commercial flights had also skyrocketed, and the convenience of flying was slowly slipping away.

With new interstate highway systems lacing our land, I found I could make a far more convenient trip by driving, even though it took longer. Of course, on trips of more than a thousand miles, I continued to fly.

During the latter part of 1980, I began to feel poorly a great deal of the time. I didn't notice this at first because on many occasions I was tired from traveling and losing sleep, but now I even found it difficult to operate when I acquired adequate rest. After eight or nine hours of sleep, I felt logy and void of energy. It was not really disturbing to think I had completely worn out my body and was nearing the end of my earthly existence because of traveling and maintaining the Youth Homes. I had often told people when I was warned about "burning myself out" that "I would rather burn out than rust out."

When I found myself constantly nauseated and losing my meals, I knew there was something else wrong, but I couldn't diagnose my problem. I realized that if I didn't have any real symptoms to show or tell the doctors, they could not find out what my problem was because my vital signs were in order and fairly normal. This condition continued through the winter months of 1980; by the time the Christmas holidays rolled around, I was glad to get off the road and have a time of rest.

14

Down but Not Out

My illness, whatever the cause, did not subside during the
Christmas holidays of 1980, but I soon had another serious problem to concern me.

Sometime before six o'clock on the morning of Saturday, January 3, 1981, Glenda and I heard a clamor at the door and men
shouting, "Fire! Fire!" Looking out the window, we saw that the
building behind our home, which housed the Garrett Apartment,
our offices, and the Hugo Meyer Cottage, was ablaze. The men
were hunters who had been driving past on the highway; they had
noticed the fire and rushed to the complex to warn anyone who
might be asleep inside. Because no one responded, they hurried
to the Big House and roused Glenda and me.

One of the hunters ran to the nearby home of staff members
Eddie and Betty Burris to call the police and fire departments,
then with the other hunters helped awaken the boys who were
sleeping in other cottages.

The following Thursday, the *Vidalia Advance* newspaper
headlined the story: YOUTH HOME ADMINISTRATION
BUILDING DESTROYED BY FIRE/"WITH GOD'S HELP

WE WILL TURN LOSS INTO GAIN.'' Excerpts from Kitty Martin Peterson's account described what we faced:

> Fire trucks arrived promptly and the damage was contained, but fire fighters, including volunteer firemen, were unable to save the administration building, which was already gutted.
>
> By daylight the schoolroom and office had become charred open spaces with twisted bits of metal as the only remains of furniture. A mass of blackened records and partially burned magazines served as a chilling reminder of what was, but what is no more.
>
> Lost were records of the boys who have been at the Home since it opened almost twenty years ago, the mailing list of friends and donors . . . slide presentations and films used in programs and lectures, and an irreplaceable collection of photographs. Also lost was the file containing all newspaper and magazine articles concerning Paul and the Home. . . .

Though not mentioned in the newspaper account, financial records were saved, thanks to the fact they were at our accountant's office in town. The article speculated that the fire resulted from the fraying of electrical wiring insulation by squirrels that abound in our pecan grove. I was quoted as follows: ''The Paul Anderson Youth Home is the Lord's work and He is in complete control of everything. We believe He wants us to have this facility, and we aren't worried about it. We have faith that He will supply our needs.''

Truett Andrew, director of curriculum and academic counselor, expressed the view of other staff members and the boys: ''We will continue, and with God's help, we will turn this loss into a gain.''

When news of the fire reached our alumni, donors, and other

friends, calls began pouring in asking what they could supply. Even many strangers wanted to help. We indeed believed God would supply our needs, since this was His work; as the weeks and months passed, donations of equipment and funds came in, allowing us to rebuild the destroyed building at a cost of approximately two hundred thousand dollars.

Thus our loss was indeed turned into a gain. During the years since 1981, the Youth Home has become stronger than ever; supporters have faithfully stood by us, and God has given us many new friends, compensating for the fact that I can no longer go out on fund-raising missions.

As I entered 1981, not only did my nausea and discomfort continue but I also began to pass large kidney stones. Now at last I had an idea what my problem was, and each time a marble-sized jagged stone passed I had a feeling of relief and joy that my problems were over. However, this feeling of euphoria was quite short-lived, because in only a matter of minutes I would feel another stone fall into my urinary tract. This went on for several weeks, and I counted over a dozen of these large stones.

On one trip to Florida, I thought I was reaching the end of my rope because the particular "boulder" I was carrying at the time completely blocked my urinary passage. For several hours, I was in great pain as I drove the five hundred miles back home. I was finally able to pass this large stone the next day, so I experienced another short period of grace.

It was on Saturday afternoon, March 14, 1981, that I headed for South Carolina to preach at a revival service that had been booked for almost a year. In fact, I had done the same program exactly a year before in a different location. It was for a church's district youth meeting, and this time parents as well as children were invited. I would have canceled the engagement if it had not been for the tremendous success I had experienced the previous year. When the invitation had been given at the end of that first service, the Holy Spirit moved scores of young people to the altar for prayer and decision.

Surprisingly, I made the twelve-hour round-trip with a minimum of discomfort, and I returned home very early the next morning. The great difficulty began about three hours later when I was awakened by the old familiar calling. Once again, I had to try and pass a stone. This time I was far from successful. It was just too large and would not pass. I had a local doctor meet me at the hospital, and after quite a struggle he was able to crush the rock and clear the passage. He asked me if I would let him take some X rays, and I knew in my heart exactly what they would show.

Soon a concerned physician approached me with the X-ray films and pointed out that hundreds of stones covered my kidneys and the passages leading from them. The immediate question was not why the stones had formed but how was I living with all of these obstructions in this vital part of my body? How could I be in such good health otherwise and keep going? The pain alone should have been excruciating enough to put me into some type of convulsion.

After consultation, doctors in Vidalia advised that I go to a center where kidney surgery and the removal of stones was a specialty. They recommended Bowman Gray Baptist Hospital in Winston-Salem, North Carolina, where I could be treated by some of the world's best urologists. They took only emergency cases, I was informed, since they were in such demand.

On Monday, March 16, arrangements were made for me to be admitted to the North Carolina hospital. A local firm generously volunteered an airplane to fly me with my party the three hundred-plus miles to Winston-Salem. Upon our arrival Tuesday after-noon, several doctors greeted me and, after viewing my X rays, said they were fully convinced I needed immediate treatment. Unfortunately, a now popular technique called extracorporeal lithotripsy, in which ultrasound shock waves are used to fragment kidney stones into powder that can easily be passed out of the body, was available then only in Munich, Germany.

For the next six weeks, I went through procedures and surgery that most people can hardly believe when I describe my experi-ences. All told, doctors performed more than twenty-four hours of professional procedures to extract the stones, some unusually large. My faith in God was certainly called on to the fullest degree. I did not have a great deal of anxiety concerning my condition, because I completely put it in the hands of the Lord. However, I felt somewhat guilty since I was requiring so much attention from my family and staff, who, as a result, were having to neglect matters back at the Home.

My most anxious moments came each night when Glenda left to return to her motel after being with me throughout the day. I knew she had to walk several blocks to her car, which was in a dark parking lot. I constantly prayed for her until she reached her room and phoned me. Our Lord traveled with Glenda each time she made the nightly trip during those six weeks. Once again, it shows that He is good and will not put more on us than we can stand.

After the first minor operation was performed to relieve one kidney and allow it to function more freely, I felt better. My appetite picked up, which indicated to me that the poison was leaving my body.

I could not ask for any better treatment or respect from doctors, nurses, and all others connected with this large medical center.

The only problem I had that was disturbing, besides the discomfort of the surgery, was emotional. I began to see my well-toned, muscular body deteriorating, though I realized this was a temporary condition because I had previously suffered weight loss during illness. I knew I had the knowledge to rebuild my body quite rapidly, but my hang-up was that my surgery had just begun. If I could see loose skin hanging from my arms now, what would it be like after all the surgeries were completed? This caused me to develop a desire to do some type of exercise while in the hospital. Naturally, there had to be a few days between my operations, even though my two major kidney surgeries were held in record time, as far as the lapsed period between the two procedures was concerned.

As I went into the operating room for the second time, I looked up at the ceiling to once again observe the beautiful pictures and paintings they had placed there; they were more attractive than a bare ceiling! I thought of the possibility that I might not survive. In regard to my personal relationship with Jesus Christ, I had no fear of going from this world into the next, but I thought about all of my obligations and the tasks I would leave undone. I also remember the hundreds of individuals around the country who had been notified of my illness. I knew that many were praying right then and would be doing so throughout my surgery. This gave me a tremendous amount of peace and brought my anxiety down to a fraction of what it ordinarily would have been.

When I came out of a deep sleep after the operation, I checked all my reflexes and made sure I had not suffered any side effects such as a stroke or surgical nerve damage. I thanked God for my condition; back in my room hours later, I had a nurse help me out of bed, and I stood up leaning against a chair, pushing it ahead of me as a kind of walker. By the next day I was doing a type of push-up against the front of my bed as I stood there, and I was also rolling my head on a pillow placed against the edge of a table, a common and widely used neck exercise. This did more for me mentally than it did physically. I simply could not stand by and bid farewell to all of the muscle tissue and conditioning I had built through the years.

I also tried to walk as much as I could but found that being weakened also gave me a greater problem in my hip joints, which were experiencing the arthritic condition triggered by the 1954 automobile accident.

After word got out that I was in the hospital, various publications and the news media wanted to interview me. I was willing to do this, but I balked when it came to pictures or video for television news. I am sure the contrast would have made a good story, but pride kept me from submitting to this at that time. I also realize that I allowed my imagination to run away with me concerning my weight loss and absence of muscle tone. I recognized this one day when I said something to Glenda about being emaciated, and she burst into laughter. She said I was larger than anyone else in North Carolina; how could I call myself "emaciated"?

All in all, I think I did well to leave the hospital six weeks after I was admitted. I was able to walk and get in and out of John Shea's airplane, which he sent for my transportation back to Vidalia. (John has been an unselfish friend and generous PAYH supporter and partner for many years; he is president of his Atlanta-based Shea and Company. John has faithfully served on our board of trustees and has been board chairman since 1986.)

After the hour-and-a-half plane ride, I found I was a little fatigued, and when I returned to my familiar surroundings, I became aware of just how much strength I had lost. This should not have been a surprise because not only had I recognized that my muscle tone was slipping away but also the countless hours of surgery and depletion of blood supply had taken their toll. Although I had tried to exercise, the many hours lying flat on my back also made me weak. Merely staying in bed will take away a certain amount of strength from anyone. When I reached the back steps of our main dwelling at the Youth Home, I found that I had to use both hands on the rail to negotiate the seven steps to the back door.

I knew from common sense and the instructions I received from my surgeon that I had to take it easy as far as lifting was concerned. I neither wanted to tear my incisions nor stretch the scar tissue around them, because I understood that the stretched scar tissue would never return to its original length and form. My endurance was just as low as my strength in general, so I was even handicapped in this way. Because of my hip condition, I could not do some of the walking and other exercises I ordinarily would have included in my activities.

In giving my entire situation thought and prayer, I came up with the idea of first performing most of my exercise routines in a hot tub. I had a very adequate one, measuring six feet by eight feet with a depth of four feet. This included three strong jets at different levels. My first thought was to buy some type of exercise bicycle and immerse the bicycle in the tub and take advantage of the hot water while pedaling the bike. As I did this, my circulation would work about twice as efficiently and, in turn, get oxygen to my starved tissue much faster. I tried it, and it worked. When this was successful, I figured there were other routines I could do in the hot tub that would allow me to strengthen my entire body.

The longer I thought and worked on ideas, the less room I

found in the tub. It came to the point where I had to devise different exercises. The ultimate was a rack I placed over the tub, which allowed me to do an exercise like half knee bends by lifting one end of the rack. The other end of the rack was stationary, and my bar was near that end. The weights were on the other end, and this gave me tremendous leverage. I did not have to use much time changing weights because I could put a minimum amount of poundage on one end and lift a maximum weight from the other.

As the days passed, I could see my strength coming back and also observed my muscles regaining their tone. I still had a lot of time on my hands, though I spent hours in the classroom teaching the boys and especially conducting Bible study. I had been on the road for twenty years or more, and abstaining from travel gave me a lot of extra time. As I began to look into my files, I was first shocked and then delighted to see how much material I had accumulated through the years just by keeping notes and making memos on cassette tapes. I had the contents for scores of books and courses that needed to be written. I also had information I wanted to record and offer interested individuals as recorded instructions and entertainment.

With my working out and finding time, after all these years, to use the notes I had made from over thirty years of training and traveling, my schedule filled up. My mind grew much more tranquil through having this challenge; I was receiving great fulfillment in knowing that soon I would be able to offer these new courses and books. I had also previously planned and was now carrying out my intentions to update my autobiography.

I continued to receive engagement requests, so I started filling a few of the ones that were relatively nearby. This was June, and I figured by October or November I should be able to accept some more distant invitations.

God had taken away my tremendous traveling ability and my schedule on the road, at least temporarily. In its place, He had given me writing and recording to do. You see, He never takes anything away unless He gives something even better. This is why I was excited about what the future held. I was able to reecho the saying, "I do not know what the future holds, but I know who holds the future!"

15

Our Walk in the Valley of the Shadow of Death

By Glenda Anderson

After Paul's health started failing in the late seventies, I began to feel a terrible emptiness. I had prayed the best I knew how, but Paul continued to experience more and more pain. Then came his horrible bout with kidney stones, which he has recounted. Talk of impending "end stage renal failure" gave me the feeling that without God's intervention, Paul might not be with us for many more years.

I struggled to commune with our heavenly Father and seek His face, but at the same time I found myself becoming bitter and resentful toward Him. How could He allow my precious husband to suffer so horribly when Paul's every effort had been to carry on the ministry to which God had called us? He had been speaking and giving lifting demonstrations more than five hundred times each year to bring in enough money to hold together our work with troubled teenagers.

God seemed far off, and I began to abandon my times of crying to Him. I shared my feelings with Paul, whose reply was then and continued to be: "This is God's business; we can request, but He may not always give us the answer we want; He loves us, and He knows what is best for us. So we must keep a definite line of communication open and allow the Holy Spirit to guide us as we travail and make our requests.''

I am so thankful that at this time I could not see what lay ahead for us in the next few years. When Paul was hospitalized eighteen times and I watched him eventually drop from 365 pounds to an unbelievable 160 pounds, God was to teach me so very, very much. I would not have believed I could withstand all that was on the threshold of my life—it would have been devastating. Thus, our Creator, in His love, allowed me to see the road ahead only by degrees.

Paul had abandoned his public lifting exhibitions in the late seventies, as he mentioned earlier, because of the intense pain and difficulty he experienced in walking due mainly to hip and spine damage suffered in the car accident in 1954 and in some degree to hereditary arthritis. His mother and other family members had suffered from rheumatoid arthritis, but in later years; this crippling disease came on Paul when he was only in his mid-forties. On top of Paul's health problems, both of us faced grief in the late seventies: he lost his mother, and I, my stepmother.

On June 10, 1982, our daughter Paula's sixteenth birthday, I noticed that Paul was exceptionally sleepy, and he was experiencing extreme nausea, unable to keep down food or liquid. By the time we admitted him to our local hospital, he could not communicate clearly. His condition, I was told, required emergency dialysis. Physicians made an opening in his peritoneal cavity, where fluids were sent in and taken out to remove the poisons.

Paul became lucid after two or three days of this. I rejoiced, but then came the dreaded news: ''Mrs. Anderson, your husband has end stage renal failure.'' I will never forget those words. They sounded so final, as if there were no hope.

It was at this point I really moved into a deeper relationship with the Lord Jesus and began to look to Him with all my heart. I did not understand why Paul had to endure such pain, but I started to experience peace: Like Paul, I believed God was in control and working out His plan in our lives.

Paula, whose childlike faith often put me to shame, continued to reach for answers in her prayer time. She said she knew God wasn't going to take her daddy; He was still going to use him because he was a good man and he loved Jesus. When I shared this with Paul, he told me to try and help her understand that, whatever God did, it was what was best, for God doesn't always choose to give healing. Paul was concerned that, should he leave us, Paula's faith would be shattered since she had such confidence that God was going to allow her daddy more time on earth.

On June 25 we admitted Paul to Talmadge Hospital (now Medical College of Georgia Hospital) in Augusta, a hundred miles north of Vidalia, and I took up residence in a nearby motel. Paul was quickly introduced to dialysis machines for life-sustaining treatment.

After about two weeks in Augusta, we returned home and began a routine of visiting a rural dialysis unit some thirty miles away three times a week. Here Paul sat in a small curtained-off area for up to four hours as the hemodialysis machine filtered waste products from his blood that passed from the shunt in an artery in his arm and back into an adjacent artery through another thin tube. He could watch television or read but was inclined to sleep because of fatigue. During the many months he was on dialysis, my precious husband was hospitalized three times with complications related to the dialysis procedure. For almost two years, he was sick to the point of regurgitating every single day. It was during this period that I saw Paul waste away from 365 pounds to an emaciated 160 pounds. A newspaper photograph of Paul sitting on the side of his bed revealed to fans and friends across the nation that indeed the World's Strongest Man had fallen on extremely difficult times.

Looking back, I see these painful days as times when my husband and I shared very special moments. Though on many occasions Paul was too ill to have conversation, there were some discussions that were especially meaningful. He shared his thoughts and plans concerning how to improve our ministry to boys, should he not live to see them implemented. We discussed what he desired for Paula and me. Then there were the times he worried so much about being a burden or that he wasn't the husband, father, or leader he wanted to be. Strangely enough, during all of this I always felt secure and convinced that Paul could still handle whatever arose, including making all the major decisions.

When it was evident that he could not continue on hemodialysis, Paul and I talked it over and decided he should go on peritoneal dialysis, which we understood was more tolerable for some people. Because this method periodically flushes the body and is faster than hemodialysis, a patient may eat and drink almost anything he wants.

Thus in late January 1983, Paul entered the Augusta hospital again. A surgeon made a small incision in his abdominal wall and threaded a thin plastic tube into the abdomen. During treatments, a special fluid flowed slowly into the peritoneal space between the inner and outer layers of the sac that lined the abdominal walls. Waste products that seeped from the abdomen into the fluid were extracted along with excess water.

For a time Paul's condition improved, though he still experienced nausea. After returning to Vidalia in February, we felt quite freed up from going to the dialysis center. However, a month after beginning the peritoneal dialysis, Paul developed peritonitis, and it was back to Augusta. His surgeon removed the peritoneal device and drained blood and fluid from his peritoneal cavity, after which antibiotics were administered. The incision in his abdomen was not sewn up but left to heal naturally, and he resumed hemodialysis.

Back home between trips to the dialysis center, Paul, in his weakened condition, was rarely awake; when he was, he often didn't feel like talking, yet I heard him continue to praise God. I began to sense that we were approaching our final weeks together. He simply could not continue to live in this condition.

In March 1983, we returned to Augusta for a series of tests; while there he contracted pneumonia, which was so severe that it required treatment with a strong mycin antibiotic.

Three weeks later, when my dear husband was able to return home, he found it difficult to stand or walk without falling. Tests showed that the mycin medication had destroyed the nerve endings in his ears, which brought on vertigo and loss of his ability to hear high-pitched sounds.

Though medical people we had seen had not recommended that Paul consider a kidney transplant, I had been trying to become knowledgeable on the subject. I had even gone to a lecture given by a renowned doctor from Pittsburgh and was extremely impressed. As Paul's condition worsened, the *Atlanta Journal/ Constitution* published an article about Paul that Jim Dezell, an executive with IBM in Atlanta, read. This triggered his phoning and later visiting us in the Augusta hospital to urge him to try a kidney transplant instead of relying on dialysis. Jim related how he had been given a new lease on life five years earlier by undergoing a kidney transplant at the University of Minnesota Hospital. He recommended that we contact Dr. John Najarian, the surgeon who had performed his transplant.

Paul's sister, Dorothy Johnson, had already indicated a desire to give Paul a kidney if he should want a transplant. She and her husband, Julius, had talked about it after they saw a television drama, "A Gift of Love," in which a man in his twenties gave his younger brother a kidney. Julius not only sanctioned his wife's unselfish desire to give Paul one of her kidneys but he was also enthusiastic about Dot's willingness to be a donor. In time Dorothy came to Augusta to undergo tests, and doctors found that there was a good half match in Dot's and Paul's kidneys, which created a green-light situation.

With this exciting news, I asked the Lord for direction as I approached Paul about taking this crucial step. My heart almost broke when I heard his reply: "Honey, I have to leave it up to you now. I'm not capable of making a decision. Whatever you want to do is okay with me."

At that moment I felt terribly alone. I sought my Savior for comfort and guidance. During the next hours I felt His warm, abundant love in a way I had never known. I now realized what I had to do.

The day was Thursday, April 21, 1983. Paul had been back in the Augusta hospital since April 11. I called Vidalia and asked our staff family to pray that God would prepare Dr. Najarian for my phone call and that He would strengthen me to present Paul's case without my breaking down. In recent years, we had experienced a few upsetting encounters with seemingly uncaring medical people, and I had no idea how Dr. Najarian might react when I called him. I was afraid if he did not receive me with discernible sensitivity, I would not make it through the conversation, because I was calling him completely cold.

God certainly prepared my way. Dr. Najarian was not in when I telephoned, but he kindly returned my call. He knew of Paul, and he had been updated on Paul by our new friend, Jim Dezell. I immediately sensed that Dr. Najarian was a patient listener, for during our approximately twenty-minute conversation he asked for additional details. At the conclusion of the call, his response caused my heart to leap with both grief and joy: "Mrs. Anderson, it sounds as if your husband is dying; please get him here as quickly as you can." He gave me necessary information and said he would be waiting to hear the details of our arrival plans.

After the conversation, I prayed as I went into action. PAYH board member Don Carter, a Texan, the son of Mary Crowley, a dear friend and founder of Home Interiors and Gifts, Inc., kindly offered to make his Falcon jet available for the trip from Augusta to Minneapolis. There were numerous details that had to be completed, including obtaining a complete medical history that our devoted nephrologist in Augusta, Dr. Jim Hudson, promised to work on overtime and deliver for the flight on Monday morning.

On Thursday night as I sat in Paul's hospital room, God directed me to read James 5:14, 15 (TLB):

> Is anyone sick? He should call for the elders of the church and they should pray over him and pour a little oil upon him, calling on the Lord to heal him. And their prayer, if offered in faith, will heal him. . . .

On two other occasions this passage had come to our attention, but in our pride we had shied away from calling on church leaders to come to pray for Paul. We prayed for others, but we would not burden others to pray for our hurts; we could do our own praying. Now God was about to teach us a great lesson.

After reading the passage in Paul's room, I was in a dilemma. I looked over at the man who had been my earthly security for almost twenty-five years, who had been my everything—my partner in life, my partner in ministry, and my best friend. He lay there in a state that rendered him unable to make a decision, and all decisions fell on me.

The Holy Spirit brought the Scripture passage to my mind again that night as I was saying my last prayer before retiring. "Lord, if this is of You," I prayed, "when I walk into Paul's room tomorrow morning, let this be the first thought I have. Empower me to share this with Paul and make him receptive. Yet, Lord, if this is my trying to bargain with You, if I am trying to make a deal with You about saving my husband's life, reveal that to me and let me never again think of calling in elders."

As I walked into Paul's hospital room the next morning, God laid it on my heart to speak to Paul about the directive in James. Paul was so dear but terribly weak and hardly knew what I was saying. However, it was as though when I began to discuss the proposition, he became more alert and said in a whisper, "Honey, everything is in your hands now, and I'm willing for anything. I have no pride left; whatever God wants is fine with me. Whatever you feel the Lord is telling you to do, please do it."

On Sunday afternoon, four of the godliest men I knew came to Augusta. Paula and I left the room while they anointed Paul and prayed over him; it was not a bargaining session but an act of obedience to the biblical command. When these men completed their mission, they came out into the hall and prayed with Paula and me. What a blessing! That day I began to see a transformation in Paul. The infection that ravaged his body had caused him to be drowsy most of the time, but now he awakened.

Paul said he had, in a supernatural way, felt Satan cast from his hospital room, and he could feel a renewing strength. We knew that we had finally humbled ourselves before Christ; we had reached the point of tearing away false pride. We were willing for whatever God wanted, and we would glory in His decision, although it could be that He might not choose to heal Paul. This could be a preparation for him to leave us. With that understanding, Paul and I both felt more peace, hope, and joy than we had known for years.

On Monday we flew Paul, still with his abdomen totally open from side to side following his peritonitis surgery, to Minneapolis, and soon we met Dr. Najarian at the University of Minnesota Hospital.

Paul felt especially comfortable with John Najarian. He was not only a skilled surgeon but also a giant of a man, obviously an athlete—a former star football player at Stanford University. Paul and I understood that at the time he was one of two surgeons in the United States who were authorized to use the drug Sandimmune or cyclosporine, which, as is now generally known, not only improves the success of kidney transplants but also helps patients recover more quickly. The drug, which suppresses the body's immune system and fights germs and other "invaders," is widely used today to help prevent transplant rejection, as recently reported in *USA Today*. With the immune system restricted in its functions, patients must rely on antibiotics to ward off infection and disease. This has been the case with Paul in recent years.

After numerous tests, and with Dr. Najarian already aware that the tests previously given Dorothy and Paul in Augusta were positive, we returned home to allow Paul to further recuperate from his bout with peritonitis and regain some strength before undergoing the transplant, which was scheduled for June 1.

A year earlier a Toccoa resident, Alethea Matuch, had begun work on an impressive monument to honor its native son, Paul, of whom Toccoans were extremely proud. Thus a sixteen-ton granite marker capped with an Olympic torch had been erected. The monument lists his birthplace as 912 East Tugalo Street in Toccoa, mentions his greatest lift of 6,270 pounds, and states that he was a 1956 Olympic gold medalist and founder of our Youth Home. The inscription concludes with a message that thrilled Paul when he read it:

ALL OUR STRENGTHS COME FROM GOD:
TO ACHIEVE—TO EXCEL—TO SUCCEED—
TO SERVE—TO SHARE—TO FORGIVE—
TO LIVE AND DIE—TO GAIN ETERNAL
LIFE THROUGH JESUS CHRIST

An event to honor Paul was scheduled for May 25, a week prior to the date for his transplant, and we were thankful that he was able to attend, though he was too weak to be present for the unveiling of the monument. This was Paul's first public appearance in over a year, and many of his longtime Toccoa friends had not seen him in a number of years. As we approached the Lake Louise Conference cafeteria for the evening event, a local patrolman stopped our car to turn us away because he did not recognize Paul; he apologized. No one was prepared for the dramatic change in his appearance, and many wept as they came up to speak to him. His hands had begun cramping as he shook hands with people, not surprising since cramps are very prevalent with dialysis patients. But how does the World's Strongest Man tell friends, "I am incapable of shaking hands"? I realized what was happening and asked several of our staff to explain Paul's situation to people without hurting their feelings.

Paul enjoyed the evening immensely. He actually ate heartily as Paula filled his plate twice. During the past twelve to eighteen months, Paul had eaten small amounts of food and there had rarely been an occasion when he had not regurgitated afterward. I was worried that any moment this could happen, but thankfully it didn't. I was concerned that he would not feel able to address the admiring audience, but God gave him strength. His adrenaline was up, as it had been in years past during his lifting exhibitions, and he was able to speak for a few minutes.

Where was my faith in all of this? Paul and I had prayed together that we would be strengthened by the Holy Spirit to do and say what would honor the Father, but in the flesh I was unable to let go of the terrible anxiety.

Paul Anderson's Big Day

The old stone house where Paul Anderson grew up is still standing on Tugalo Street, still shrouded by two towering oak trees. On Wednesday, in the golden sunshine of a late afternoon, they gathered under those oaks at 912 East Tugalo and remembered what Paul Anderson was, and still is. By the time the sun had set they had honored Paul Anderson, and some had wept for him.

Wednesday was Paul Anderson Day in his hometown. The older men and women knew him as a friend and neighbor. The children, like Jay Dooley, weren't quite sure what was happening. They'd seen the men working on the monument outside 912 East Tugalo for the past month, the monument to honor the "World's Strongest Man." When you're four years old, it's hard to comprehend lifting 6,270 pounds.

"He didn't really understand who Mr. Anderson was," said Jay's mother, Kathy. "He'd thought he'd get to see him today. He compared him to The Incredible Hulk and Mr. T on 'The A Team.' In his mind that's what he is. Jay thought Mr. Anderson would come and knock down the door."

Mr. Anderson was inside the stone house, but he wouldn't be opening the door, much less knocking it down.

He is 50 now and very sick. He has acute renal failure and must endure dialysis treatments twice each week. This weekend he and his sister, Dorothy Johnson, will fly to Minneapolis, where Paul will receive a kidney transplant from Dot. On Wednesday, though, Anderson was sitting in his old home, too weak to stand outside for the 15-minute ceremony to unveil his monument. . . .

At the Georgia Baptist Assembly, some 500 people attended a banquet honoring Anderson. He was already seated when they arrived. He's only 5-9, and although he weighed 375 pounds in his prime, Anderson's weight loss is startling. Slouched in his chair, he seemed dwarfed by his 16-year-old daughter, Paula, sitting beside him.

When the Stephens County High ensemble played "America the Beautiful," Anderson clapped softly. Once, his hands pounded 20-penny nails into two-by-fours, but now he applauded gingerly by tapping the base of his hands together.

Tom Landry, coach of the Dallas Cowboys and a close friend of Anderson, was the main speaker. He talked about football, and religion, and Paul Anderson. He called him "a super athlete," and a better Christian. "Paul Anderson will win the battle he's fighting right now," Landry said. "We need to hear that booming voice say, 'I won't live a day without Jesus Christ.' "

Anderson, ashen-faced, struggled to his feet and supported himself on the rostrum with forearms that were still massive. He thanked everyone, particularly his sister, his wife, Glenda, and his daughter. And then: "Even though I was the World's Strongest Man, I believe I have been more effective the last three or four weeks in my weakness. Now I'm gonna slip out early. Please forgive my staggering. It's not because of my weakness but vertigo from taking antibiotics.

"If someday you hear that Paul Anderson is dead, he's not dead. He's gone to live with God. He can't live anymore in this tired old vehicle. Don't weep for Paul Anderson."

But they were weeping for him, many of them. And when he concluded with, "Here tonight, you've proved Thomas Wolfe wrong. You can go home, my friends; thank you for bringing me home," they were standing, applauding, and crying.

When Anderson started to leave, there was a hush, a stunned, awkward silence choking the room. The World's Strongest Man balanced on a cane held in his right hand. He wrapped his left arm around Glenda's shoulders and hobbled toward an exit. It was like Toto pulling open the curtain on the Wizard of Oz. Finally, the applause resumed. At the door a man said, "Good luck." Paul Anderson nodded, then struggled into the front seat of a waiting black limousine. And then he was gone.

Condensed from article by Jack Wilkinson in the
Atlanta Journal & Constitution, May 26, 1983

On this occasion and during those difficult months, it would have been impossible, without God's Word and the comfort of the Holy Spirit, to endure Paul's suffering and the fear that gripped me. I often sought strength from the Psalms, and Psalm 18 became a lift at such times as the banquet in Toccoa, especially verses 1–3, 6 from *The Living Bible:*

> Lord, how I love you! For you have done such tremendous things for me. The Lord is my fort where I can enter and be safe; no one can follow me in and slay me. He is a rugged mountain where I hide; he is my Savior, a rock where none can reach me, and a tower of safety. He is my shield. He is like the strong horn of a mighty fighting bull. All I need to do is cry to him—oh, praise the Lord—and I am saved from all my enemies! . . . In my distress I screamed to the Lord for his help. And he heard me from heaven; my cry reached his ears.

That night in Toccoa was a beautiful encouragement to Paul, Paula, and me, as well as our Youth Home family. We felt such love!

On May 28, Don Carter flew us back to Minneapolis for the transplant. The media was wonderful. WSB television in Atlanta met us in Minneapolis and daily reported back to Georgians on Paul's and Dot's progress. God was good; all went well. Dot returned to Toccoa a week after surgery; Paul, Paula, and I came home to Vidalia approximately two weeks later. We were extremely thankful for the progress Paul was making and eternally grateful to Dot for her loving, unselfish act that had not only been such a boost to Paul's health but which had also given them a much closer and deeper awareness of their love for each other.

We went back to Minneapolis in September for Paul's three-month checkup. Everything looked really good. By March 1984, Paul's walking had improved tremendously; he had developed his endurance to a great extent and was encouraged, as we all were.

Then came a setback. I had gone to Dallas to help with the opening of a girls home, and while there I received a phone call from Paul. He had taken a terrible fall. He was accustomed to taking tumbles and, being the athlete he is, he was able to control his falls. However, this time his dog, a playful rottweiler, caused him to trip, and he hurt his lower back. X rays proved negative, but I was not to realize until he flew into Dallas that weekend just what a setback he had experienced. Paul looked extremely ill and needed a wheelchair. After the injury healed, his walking worsened, and he barely managed with a walker he had designed that had small eight-inch wheels. When he traveled, he relied on a wheelchair.

In May 1984, Paul spoke at our daughter's high school graduation, where for the first time he allowed the public in Vidalia to see him in a wheelchair. I was extremely proud of him. God was so good, having given Paul an extension on his earthly life through the transplant. I thought of the words of David:

> I will praise you to all my brothers; I will stand up before
> the congregation and testify of the wonderful things you
> have done. . . . I will publicly fulfill my vows in the pres-
> ence of all who reverence your name.
>
> Psalm 22:22, 25 (TLB)

In the fall of 1984, when we were rejoicing at Paul's progress, we faced another nightmare situation. I had recently returned home after taking Paula back to Liberty University in Lynchburg, Virginia, following a weekend visit with us. She had become ill with a stomach virus that had attacked me a few days previously.

The symptoms were excruciating stomach cramps. On October 26, I found that Paul was also suffering severe stomach pains, and after checking with his doctor, I began administering to Paul the same medication I had taken, for I assumed he had contracted the same virus. I reasoned that, immunosuppressed, he would be highly susceptible to any germ with which he came in contact.

By Saturday morning, his condition had worsened. Blood tests revealed no clue to his illness; even his hemoglobin count was improved, though later we were to learn that often hemoglobin elevates during dehydration. By late Saturday morning, doctors believed he could be bothered by a kidney stone—devastating news, for his transplanted kidney could be in jeopardy.

Paul was in such excruciating pain by this time that only powerful medication could relieve him, and it did not help until about seven o'clock Sunday morning. By midmorning, he seemed to be resting comfortably. I felt this was good for him, since he had not been able to really rest for three or four days. I constantly checked on him that afternoon, and he appeared to be sleeping peacefully. Many times in the past when he had hurt so horribly with arthritis, he would sleep almost around the clock from sheer exhaustion. Because of this, I felt good about his remaining asleep all day.

That evening I phoned Paula at school to tell her that her daddy was finally resting, and at about eleven o'clock I went to bed. My head had just hit the pillow when I remembered that Paul had not taken his prednisone and cyclosporine, the antirejection medications so vital to a kidney transplant patient. I hastened to awaken Paul, but he gave little response. I realized almost instantly that something was terribly wrong, and I called Eddie Burris, the young man we think of as our son who joined our staff in 1970 after his graduation from the Youth Home. Eddie was there within minutes, as was Truett Andrew, our closest friend and co-worker.

By this time, we all knew that there was no awakening Paul, though at one moment he began begging for water but seemed unable to swallow.

I asked Truett to call an ambulance while Eddie and I continued to minister to Paul. Inside, I was frightened beyond what I thought I was capable of bearing. I wanted to run, die, anything but deal with this hurt and anxiety. My stomach was in knots, and I felt as if my heart were in my mouth. Through all of the trauma we had known in the past three years, this was certainly the worst. My Lord had previously surrounded me with His loving strength, and I knew He would again. I began to pray as I cared for Paul, asking God to touch him and carry me through one moment at a time.

At the hospital, Paul's vital signs gave little hope, Dr. Reddy Kalathoor informed me. He was Paul's local physician, who had been kept well informed of Paul's condition since the transplant surgery.

I phoned the transplant office in Minneapolis and soon was talking with Barb Elick, head of the department. I told her it was our impression that the problem was related to the kidney, possibly rejection or infection.

"Glenda, it sounds really bad. How far is your nearest large hospital where there would be a doctor who is accustomed to handling transplant patients?"

All such hospitals were hours away, and we agreed the best move would be to fly him to Minneapolis, about a three-hour trip. I wanted no strangers to touch that kidney! I knew if Paul lost it, he would prefer death.

"Glenda, we will have a team waiting. Bring him as quickly as you can. I just hope it isn't too late," Barb said.

As it turned out, a plane could not get into Vidalia because of fog, and we had to rush Paul by ambulance to Savannah. All city police en route and the highway patrol were alerted, and we made the eighty-five-mile dash in a little more than an hour. About half-past eight Monday morning, Paul was wheeled into the emergency room. He had been totally unconscious since leaving Vidalia. The young emergency medical team who had accompanied us from Savannah told me they had revived Paul after his heart stopped twice on the way to the hospital from the airport.

Five doctors and several nurses worked for a few minutes with him and gave bleak reports. Then Dr. Najarian, the man God had already so dramatically used in our lives, arrived. I felt just as I did the first time I brought Paul to him; it was as though I knew I could give my precious husband over to his care and let go. I felt confident that he was God's man for Paul's needs.

After examining him, even Dr. Najarian, who is always an optimist, said, "I don't believe he will make it through an operation. He doesn't seem strong enough this time to pull it off." Dr. Najarian said that surgery was the only hope, for it was either Paul's colon or gallbladder; peritonitis was threatening his life, and he had to have immediate surgery.

After Paul was in the operating room, I had to decide whether to immediately phone Paula at Liberty University or wait for the results of the surgery before calling. I wanted so much to be with Paula, a real daddy's girl, and comfort her, but it wasn't possible. Then Truett related to me that she had just phoned Vidalia and learned a news bulletin had gone out on the Georgia Network News that Paul had returned to Minnesota in critical condition. Some radio stations in north Georgia had reported there was an indication that Paul had died.

Believing that Paula might somehow hear about her daddy, I called her immediately. Thanks to our wonderful friend John Shea, who once again made available his private jet, Paula was soon at my side, along with Betty Burris, Eddie's wife.

Paula was crushed, but she also knew her Sustenance. She asked many of her friends, acquaintances, and professors at Liberty University to pray for her daddy. Although she suffered stomach cramps caused by anxiety during her trip to us and was extremely emotional, she still drew claim on her faith, believing and praying that God would touch and spare her daddy. We phoned Christian friends across the nation to join us in prayer.

About two o'clock Dr. Najarian came into the family waiting room to report that the surgery was over. The colon had ruptured, and infection had spread over most of Paul's body. For a time, his abdomen was left completely open in order for the poison to drain out. Dr. Najarian said Paul had about a 20 percent chance of survival. If he did make it, he probably would lose his transplanted kidney.

I did not really know how to pray. The Lord brought to my mind the truth in Romans 8:26, which says that the Holy Spirit intercedes for us when we do not know how to pray. Dialysis for Paul was a tormented quality of life. It would be disastrous for him to lose his only functioning kidney.

I knew if Paul could have his choice, he would far prefer to go on and be with Jesus. I vividly recalled the times during the period he was on dialysis that he would pray for the Lord to have mercy on him and take him to Glory. As I pondered Dr. Najarian's words, I gave over to the Holy Spirit's intercession. I wanted complete healing for Paul. It was so terribly hard to ask God to make me willing to let him go; I could not comprehend life without him. However, during those long months he was on dialysis when I thought there seemed to be no hope for a better life, I learned to live one day at a time with physical death in the shadows.

The first few days after surgery, Paul remained in a deep coma as he lay in his bed in the Transplant ICU at Station 22 with around-the-clock nurses. He would change expressions, but his eyes remained shut. The third day he was moved to Station 44, the Septic Unit. He had five different infections; we were given no encouragement. Daily, we praised the Lord for just one more day and diligently prayed for the seemingly dormant kidney.

About the fifth or sixth day, Paul responded to Paula by squeezing her hand, and a short while later he opened his eyes, joining the world of the conscious. Whether the kidney would pick up its pace or not was still to be seen. Hemodialysis continued to be necessary. We anxiously watched Paul's chemistries and constantly prayed that each day would bring more voluntary volume from the sixty-year-old transplanted organ. At the end of the second week, Paul was moved back to Station 22, the Transplant ICU. The kidney was holding its own, producing enough volume for us to know it had not shut down.

Around this time, we remembered to again lay claim to the promises of James 5. At my request, Dr. Arvid Kingsriter, an area minister whose son, Doug, was a former Minnesota Vikings player Paul had known through the Fellowship of Christian Athletes, came to Paul's room and laid hands on him, anointed him with oil, and prayed that God would restore his kidney to its full function. Subsequently, we saw an almost immediate, drastic change. The Holy Spirit had prayed for me in my deepest hour of despair, and now our loving heavenly Father had given us another miracle.

All of this seems so supernatural, and yet, according to God's Word, it is very natural for those of us who seek to live by complete faith. It is not always God's will to heal; we must remember that. Our prayer was that the Lord would give Paul a few more years to serve Him. We desperately wanted to minister to more teenagers and teach others how to successfully work with their particular age group by sharing with them the wisdom and knowledge God has given us through the years since we established the Youth Home. God has blessed this work in a phenomenal way, allowing us to see many, many lives changed when we have implemented the methods of guidance He has imparted to us.

Paul left the hospital the last week of November, following four weeks of care, with a healthy kidney and a colostomy that was his companion until we returned to Minneapolis in January 1985.

Since 1985, Paul has been hospitalized three additional times; first for hip replacements and on two other occasions for treatment and surgery, much of which related to the injury he sustained in the 1954 automobile accident, which also resulted in nerve damage to his lower spine. Due to these problems, plus the destruction of inner ear nerve endings, resulting in his loss of balance, and medication side effects, Paul is not mobile, and he probably will never be, though I daily pray that God will enable him to walk again. There has been some improvement in his balance and strength in his legs. For example, there was a time when, if a leg fell off his bed, he couldn't pull it back up; recently I rejoiced that he was able to pull a leg from the floor straight up and lay it back on the bed. This was a result of his intensive exercise program, which has enabled him to build himself up to approximately 250 pounds of muscle and bone.

Paul exercises from six to eight hours every day on a weight machine: he lies on a table working with weights attached to pulley cables; this strengthens his legs and back. He probably works out more now than during his weightlifting prime, more than a healthy twenty-year-old would. He plays all of this down because, although he is grateful for the progress he has made, he feels he still has a long way to go. "One of my biggest problems," he says, "is physically wanting to be twenty-five though I am approaching sixty!"

Paul's role at the Home is much as it has always been; just his mere presence gives us the strength of leadership that we need. His voice is as strong as ever. He handles much of the Youth Home correspondence by dictating on a cassette recorder. We have a rather sophisticated type of walkie-talkie system that allows him to keep in touch with all of us. Paul brings the Sunday message most of the time.

His eating habits are much as they were in the years he enjoyed good health; some of his medications render him nauseous, and this curtails his appetite. He doesn't really eat a lot, even when he feels well. About five o'clock in the afternoon he has his main meal, often consisting of several small sandwiches and sometimes fish. He doesn't eat much when he awakens in the morning; however, occasionally he wants some food during the night. His favorite drink is mineral water, and it is his main source of liquid.

In May 1990, Paul was scheduled to travel to Demorest in the north Georgia Appalachian foothills to receive an honorary teaching doctorate from Piedmont College, but he was not well enough to make the trip. The honor was bestowed on him in Vidalia in July. In May, when Paul was to receive the honor, the college gave an honorary doctorate of laws to Prescott S. Bush, Jr., elder brother of President George Bush. Though small, Piedmont was cited in 1988 by *U.S. News and World Report* as one of the nation's top 125 schools. Paul was quoted in a news article as saying that he considered the honor extended to him from Piedmont "one of my greatest personal gratifications." Earlier the same month, I was awarded the Outstanding Former Student Award by the high school from which I graduated in Tallulah Falls. So May 1990 was a memorable month for both of us.

In all that we have experienced in the years of Paul's health problems, we would not trade that agony, despair, and heartbreak for anything. In moments when we both felt we could take no more, we would read passages from the Book of Job, and especially the Psalms, where we found such comfort in knowing that God doesn't leave us without a way to endure, since we belong to Him. He does not promise us that life will be easy, but He tells us He will give us strength, just as He told the Apostle Paul when he begged God to make him well again. Each time God told Paul, "No. But I am with you; that is all you need. My power shows up best in weak people" (2 Corinthians 12:9 TLB). The Apostle Paul went on to write:

> Now I am glad to boast about how weak I am; I am glad to be a living demonstration of Christ's power, instead of showing off my own power and abilities. Since I know it is all for Christ's good, I am quite happy about "the thorn,"
> . . . for when I am weak, then I am strong. . . .
> 2 Corinthians 12:9, 10 (TLB)

No words could be more relevant to my Paul, who continues to be known as the World's Strongest Man! Indeed, God has given us both the strength to endure, and He has brought us into a closer communion with Him that we never would have experienced otherwise.

Voices From the Past

March 7, 1989

Dear Paul,

I remember you from my very first FCA Conference in 1965 in Estes Park, Colorado, and have seen you several times since then. I've kept in touch whenever I could with other friends of yours such as John Lotts, Ray Hildebrand, and Jim Jeffery. All of you were really a witness for Christ to me, and I can't thank you enough for the strength that you gave me.

Paul, in your lifetime, you've done so much for other people, and while trophies and plaques and recognition can't always come, I want you to know from the bottom of my heart how much I do appreciate you. I know God has a special place for you in heaven, but that will be reserved till a later date till He finishes using you here on earth. Do hope you are feeling better, Paul.

> Your friend in Christ,
> Ken Hatfield,
> Head Football Coach
> University of Arkansas Razorbacks
> (Now head football coach, Clemson University)

February 11, 1989
Dear Paul,
We pray for you every day. The Lord has used your life for His glory for many years, and He has more assignments for you up the road. If not your legs or arms, He can use your head and your heart. You and Glenda are an inspiration to many, many friends. It's amazing what the Lord has achieved (and is achieving) through you.

Yours in Jesus,
Watson Spoelstra
(Retired Sports Editor)
St. Petersburg, Florida

April 23, 1990
Little did I realize when I helped Glenda and Paul Anderson incorporate their Youth Home what a magnificent success it would be or what a satisfying experience it would be for me.

After watching probably fifteen hundred boys, most of whom were destined for penal institutions, including penitentiaries, get their lives straightened out and emerge as good citizens with the right kind of values, I marvel at the transformations I have seen. I can assure you that, aside from the church, my close association with the Paul Anderson Youth Home has been the most satisfying experience I have had with any charitable or social organization. Having served as PAYH Board Chairman or Chairman Emeritus for these twenty-eight years gives me a genuine feeling of self-fulfillment.

May the Lord continue to bless the Home and everyone connected with it as richly in the future as He has in the past.

Sincerely,
Gerald H. Achenbach

16
Going Stronger Than Ever in Vidalia

Because of my health problems, making it almost impossible for me to travel, I have had to change hats here at the Home. Much of my outreach is by mail, and as I weigh out everything, I find my present condition is a mixed blessing. I can spend more time with the boys and give immediate help to our staff in regard to policy decisions. I can work out more to rebuild my body, though it is a big challenge for a man approaching sixty. I can catch up on many ideas I have had for producing helpful publications. Thank God I can stay busy and at the same time depend on Glenda and an excellent staff to keep the Home running smoothly.

In addition, being at the Home every day makes it possible for me to be more closely involved in decisions, and I also have more time to spend with our staff.

Though I am now pretty well confined to a wheelchair, I would love to once again walk and get around the country to spread the word about our ministry and bring in needed revenue; however, as I have previously mentioned, God has certainly continued to bless us with faithful supporters who keep us going. Finances have always been a major concern. I work diligently each day to rebuild my body in hopes of walking again, but if I never completely succeed, I will strive to be an example for others by not quitting. It is all in the hands of our Lord, whether I stay here on earth and get better for a season to witness and labor for Him, or whether He calls me home to have the undeserved privilege of being forever in His wonderful presence.

My family continues to be a joy and inspiration to me, as they have been through the years. I don't know what I would have done without the strong support Glenda has given me; continuing our ministry to boys would have been difficult without her, despite a faithful staff and board of men and women who work with us. God certainly gave me a prize when He gave me Glenda.

And what a delight our daughter, Paula, has been. A lovely, trim blonde, she graduated in 1988 from Liberty University in Lynchburg, Virginia, with a double major in public relations-journalism and psychology. She did her internship with the Michael Guido Evangelistic Association in Metter, Georgia, and then in early 1988 worked as coordinator of public relations for Edwards Baking Company of Atlanta.

On October 14, 1989, it was a privilege for me to give Paula in marriage to Edward Lamar Schaefer of Atlanta, whom she met at Liberty. The wedding took place in a garden setting in back of the Big House on our PAYH campus. I accompanied her to the altar in my wheelchair.

Paula and Edward will eventually be ministering to young people. Edward has a B.S. degree in youth ministries; Lord willing, Paula will complete her master's degree in counseling by January 1991.

In 1987, God blessed us with David Paine, a dynamic Christian doctor who specializes in internal medicine. Not only has David come to the Home daily to care for me but he has also become our close friend and PAYH physician. Recently, we were overjoyed when he accepted a position on our board of directors.

I must say that at this time, more than in any other period since the Home's inception in 1961, we can point out, with gratitude to God, numerous accomplishments. The boys we currently have in our program are some of our finest, and we are delighted that many of our alumni continue to keep in touch and visit us. They seem to realize that they received something during their stay in the Home that was unique, and they want to come back and be a part of it. Frequently, we talk on the telephone with our family members who are out in the world and enjoy their visits as they come by to spend the night or just have a meal with us.

We endeavor to send our boys away as well prepared as possible. We know they are likely to be apprehensive about leaving our structured environment, where they have lived for up to a year, but we hope that the motivation and self-confidence gained at the Home fortifies them to successfully tackle the world. We have found that an adolescent who likes himself stays out of trouble. Therefore, we strive to teach the boys here at the Home that they are very special, because God Himself made them and arranged through Jesus Christ for them to be a part of His family; He even gave them an opportunity to come to us and be part of the Paul Anderson Youth Home family. This approach has certainly paid off, as we have had boys from all over the nation who have done well in whatever field they have chosen. Thankfully, they appear to drift very little from the spiritual and moral nurturing they have been given here at the Home.

Some of our young men are now well into their forties, and we can judge their success as adults. Let me convey without equivocation that we are extremely proud of almost all our alumni. In the next chapter, you will become acquainted with some of our graduates.

Many of these young men go into the military instead of pursuing higher education right away. The reason for this is that they do not know what they would like to major in at that time in their lives, and a term in the armed services seems to clear their heads, better equipping them to choose their life vocations. Our fellows are well prepared for military service. They are already in good physical condition, which is immediately noticed by their superior officers. These young men are, of course, disciplined and do not need to be reminded how to address those of higher rank.

To our sorrow, one of our young men died in Vietnam; his name is inscribed on the Vietnam Veterans Memorial in Washington, D.C. We had many who served our country in those sad years. Along with our grief, we point with pride and humble appreciation to these young men.

In the recent past, only rarely have any of our graduates returned to juvenile or adult penal institutions. Two of our alumni were on the honor roll, according to a recent report: one in a vocational-technical school and the other in college. Not long ago, a young man who completed his advanced infantry training at Fort Benning, Georgia, was chosen as one out of his company (189 men) and one out of three in his battalion (about 1,000 men) for a special presidential force in the army's ranger unit.

Although our original goal was a boys home, we took in some girls when the Home was first started, as previously mentioned. Several of our girls continue to keep in touch and deserve recognition. For example, one of our young ladies received her master's degree and went into research work with Down's syndrome children. She had an outstanding paper published on the subject. Another of our girls has climbed the promotion ladder in a department of our Georgia state government and, through her diligence and commitment, has become quite a fine young executive.

One of our greatest joys is having our graduates return to the Paul Anderson Youth Home to serve as members of our staff; this has often been the case during the years we have been in operation. The most enduring has been a young man named Eddie Burris, who is like a son to us.

Eddie, his wife, Betty, and their two daughters, Kimberly and Blair, fit in beautifully with the Home's environment. Eddie came to us at an early age compared with our usual requirement of age sixteen or older. After graduating from high school, he went out into the world and worked awhile, then returned in the early seventies to be a real godsend as part of our staff. Eddie and Betty have responsibilities that include counseling, office work, and dozens of other tasks that any parents would handle in their own household.

At the Home, we take in the adolescent who is in trouble because of an offense against society and is usually already sentenced to a penal institution. The uniqueness of our ministry, as compared with other children's homes, is that we accept the boy who is already in detention, one in whom we can see a glimmer of hope if he is redirected, loved, and encouraged.

These are the boys who have been hurt, disappointed, and perhaps abused. They have become callous, hardened, and rebellious, so it takes daily attention and dedication to help them. We do much more than simply provide room and board; we are responsible for them twenty-four hours a day in an intensely structured and demanding environment. The goal we have set is to teach our boys to do nothing less than their best, and these teachings are always biblically based, emphasizing the instructions of our Lord and Savior, Jesus Christ.

As alluded to earlier, we can relate historical and current events to the Bible. When reading about prophecy in the Bible, we can often point to history and show the students that many of the things prophesied thousands of years ago have already happened. In current events, we can frequently show that our daily newspaper is running second best to the Scriptures, which have already told us what was going to happen. By these truths, we find that our Bible study, current events, and history/geography can complement one another.

Through our ministry these young people, who otherwise might be incarcerated for much of their lives, receive instruction to enable them to develop into solid, productive citizens. Interestingly, the Georgia Division of Youth Services reports that the daily cost per boy in Youth Development Centers is ninety-eight dollars in contrast to the Paul Anderson Youth Home's sixty-seven dollars. In other states' penal institutions, this cost per day is often higher, and we, of course, accept boys from many other states. However, there is no way to fairly equate costs since programs vastly differ; compared to state programs, we believe the Paul Anderson Youth Home offers much more, providing spiritual, mental, physical, emotional, and social guidance: rehabilitation of the total person.

How does a day go at the Youth Home? The boys usually awaken at 6:00 A.M., and they immediately make their beds and run a mile. We have a soft running course, which keeps them from injuring joints or pulling muscles. After their run, they perform their regular chores, ranging from cleaning the bathrooms in their cottages to helping prepare breakfast. We change these chores periodically so a family member will not become discouraged with one particular task.

After breakfast and the winding up of chores, including a spotless cleaning of the dining hall, our students assemble for their first class, Bible study. Next we have current events, in which we teach geography, history, and the everyday happenings in the world, with special emphasis on international hot spots. We often show the television news during this period, giving the boys further exposure to occurrences of that day.

Regular schoolwork and a great deal of tutoring fill the remainder of the day. On numerous occasions, we have brought young people through three grades of high school in ten to twelve months. Many of our tutors are volunteers who are retired teachers. They see the need and enjoy the one-to-one ratio.

To help us know what type of help our boys may need and how to assist them in their future pursuits, various tests and evaluations are administered, including the Johnson O'Connor Research Foundation's excellent aptitude tests. We emphasize special tutoring for the ASVAB, the entrance test for the armed forces. If students score well, they will have a far better choice of jobs in the military; if bonuses are being given, this enhances their eligibility for the best benefits and vocational opportunities.

We also include an individualized program of study for the SAT or college board test. By being well prepared for this exam, our youths can make higher scores and have the opportunity to enroll in the colleges of their choice.

Throughout the day, we can observe our young men in individual study carrels, studying and being tutored in addition to learning to use our computers, which enable them to prepare for the next day, the next week, year, and decade. We believe that giving our students hands-on experience with computers is important not only technologically but academically as well.

In the early evening, the fellows have free time for supervised recreation, including basketball, football, tennis, swimming, and weightlifting. Many of them choose to read, play indoor games such as Ping-Pong and pool, write letters, or study, as surprising to some as that may be.

Having started their day at 6:00 A.M., our boys are ready for bed between 10:00 and 11:00 P.M., relatively early for young men of their ages.

We do not want our fellows to grow stale by having the same

routine day after day, so we plan such change-of-pace activities as educational, recreational, and cultural field trips—called our "Horizons" program because these outings broaden the boys' horizons and develop their self-confidence. We also take our students on tours of businesses, where they can see our free-enterprise system at work, and we invite professional men and women to come in and lecture about their roles in chosen careers.

Another activity that gives us a break from the routine is the annual Onion Run during Vidalia's celebration of the famous sweet onion that originated in our small Georgia town. Our boys have done well in the Onion Run and in races held by other towns, for these young fellows are in good condition and just learn to pace themselves for the specific races they choose.

As you might guess, our Youth Home family is usually at or very near its capacity of nineteen. Since we have what I call a "rolling admission and graduation program," it is generally not long before we can take action on a new applicant. We try to keep one bed open so that in an emergency we can take a new family member or have a place for an alumnus to spend a night or two with us.

Though we are not planning to expand the Home, from time to time we become involved in building or improving. In the late 1980s, we renovated the gymnasium and added a weight room to this facility. The majority of the work was done by our boys, aided by an alumnus who is a builder. This project taught the young men valuable skills and gave them a great deal of self-confidence. They learned that no task is too large for them to handle.

The new weight room was equipped with a weight machine and other bodybuilding equipment that was primarily funded through the generosity of the father of one of our boys and many people he approached about contributing materials or monies for the project.

We have plans to expand the dining hall, which will provide more space for both dining and recreation. We added a vitally needed walk-in cooler. Previously, we sometimes had to turn down perishable food donations because we had no place to store them. The new cooler has proved to be a tremendous asset.

As I close this update on the Youth Home, I reiterate the fact that we consider this God's project. We were called into this work, and it is dedicated to Jesus Christ. We first and foremost witness for Him and believe that the range of success we have attained has been granted only because God is with us. He has given us a faithful staff and board of trustees as well as raised up loyal supporters who have undergirded us with prayer and kept the ministry going through faithful, sacrificial gifts.

After a Quarter of a Century
Serving Youth

Paul and Glenda Anderson have devoted their lives to helping young people, and their genuine Christian love and concern have been a valuable investment in the youth of our state, impacting the direction of their lives and making a real difference in their future. . . . I, Joe Frank Harris, Governor of the State of Georgia, do hereby proclaim the day of October 5, 1986, as "PAUL ANDERSON YOUTH HOME DAY" in Georgia in honor of its 25th anniversary, and do further commend Paul and Glenda Anderson for their fine Christian example and life-changing work which continues to touch and bless the lives of young people across Georgia.

Excerpt from Paul Anderson Youth Home Day Proclamation

During the past six years that I have been Judge of the Juvenile Court of Houston County, I have on numerous occasions had the opportunity to refer youths to your facility. I personally feel that your Home offers an invaluable service to the troubled children throughout Georgia and that many youths have greatly benefited from your services.

Herbert L. Wells, Judge, Houston County Juvenile Court, Warner Robins, Georgia (1986)

Several of the probation officers from Cobb County have had the opportunity to visit your facility and are excited about the work you are doing with our youth. If it were not for homes like yours that provide alternative programs, many of those young people would be filling our detention centers. We greatly appreciate the fine work you and your staff are doing.

Wayne Phillips, Judge, Juvenile Court of Cobb County, Marietta, Georgia (1986)

195

The quarter century you have dedicated to instilling your young wards with a dedication to patriotism, Christianity, and a responsible life-style continues to be so evident in your "graduates." I have personally known several fine examples of Paul Anderson youth, and we were fortunate enough to employ one of your graduates in City government this summer.

W.S. "Smitty" Snell, Mayor, Vidalia, Georgia (1986)

17
Our Graduates

Most people who go out of their way to help someone all too often receive no special word of gratitude afterward. This lack of courtesy seems to be a trend of our age, but even Jesus experienced this after healing ten lepers; only one returned to say thank you. I am glad, however, that our Paul Anderson Youth Home graduates have a good batting average when it comes to keeping in touch and showing their appreciation for the miracles the Lord performed during their tenures here.

More than fifteen hundred troubled teenage boys and approximately twenty girls have been under our care. Through the years, particularly on special occasions, Glenda and I, along with our faithful staff, are encouraged by letters, phone calls, and visits from "family" members who have graduated and gone out into the world. Some regularly show their gratitude by sending love offerings to the Home in order that other young people can have a second chance.

Particularly on Mother's Day and Father's Day, Glenda and I receive notes and cards from alumni thanking us for being mom and dad during stormy times in their formative years. A home-made card that read, "For a mom who changed my life!" brought joy to Glenda and me. Steven*, who signed his note inside the card, "Your loving accepted son," began, "On this Day, Love and Appreciation go to you because you always give kindness, joy, peace, and gentleness too!" He added: "You know when to be strict; you know when to be kind; your sweet goodness surpasses my mind!"

In another note to Glenda, Bobby penned:

> Thank you for putting up with me for thirteen months. Even my mother wanted to kick me out, but you're different; you wanted to give me a home and showed me love. I realize that I caused a lot of trouble, but you always believed in me. Happy Mother's Day. I love you.

Joy filled my heart as I read a Father's Day greeting from Devereaux:

> So many people know you for your physical strength. But what some don't know is the spiritual strength that you show all of your "sons" as they go through the program. Thank you for being such an inspiration to me spiritually and patriotically. I hope I can be such an example for my children. Have a great Father's Day.

One of the most concrete examples of appreciation has been shown by Bobby Cole, along with his family, who live on Hilton Head Island, South Carolina. Bobby was one of our "sons" back in the early seventies, and since 1976 he, his father, William, a retired vice president and general manager of operations for a popular Hilton Head resort, and brother Tom, general manager of

---

* In most instances in this chapter, surnames of graduates are omitted to protect their privacy.

another Hilton Head resort, coordinate a fun-filled weekend trip to Hilton Head for our Youth Home residents. Bobby Cole says he's helping return only a taste of what he received during his stay with us.

Bobby was quoted in the October 16, 1987, issue of the *Island Packet,* published on Hilton Head Island:

> I wasn't into violence or anything. I just wouldn't go to school. I came real close to going through the juvenile courts to reform school, but a friend of the family told us about the Paul Anderson Youth Home. It gave me a totally different outlook on life. When I went there I was full of hate, was apathetic, and had no cares, could care less about life itself. I was there less than two years, and when I left I had self-respect. I knew what responsibility was. I realized that I'm not the only human being on earth, and the world does not revolve around me; I have to learn to revolve around the world.

Besides Bobby and his family, many island businesses and individuals have given goods and services to make the annual trip to Hilton Head possible for our young men.

At times we hear from graduates who wish they had heeded our advice not to return to the old crowd and risk falling back into a troubled life-style. As I was completing the final chapters of this book, Damon, a 1985 graduate of the Home, wrote to say he was ashamed to report that he was in a drug rehabilitation center in Georgia, "because I went back home to old 'friends.' " However, Glenda and I were pleased that he asked for prayer and wanted "to be clean and live a true Christian life." Damon concluded with, "I truly love you like my own parents. You've shown me a side of life that I had never known, and that's what I'm desperately fighting to get back now." He included the following letter that he wanted us to read as a challenge to our boys:

Dear Youth Home Boys,

What I am writing here is a letter to you describing my life after graduation from the Home. First, let me say that while I was there, I put my heart and everything I had into improving my life in all the areas that the Home gives you an opportunity in which to grow. I feel I did a wonderful job in improving on these areas. The one statement I heard over and over again (and I'm sure at least some of you have heard similar statements) was, "Damon, you *do not* need to go back to your hometown where your old 'friends' are because chances are you will fall on your face. Go into the military or attend some type of school so you will not come in contact with these people." For one thing, I didn't want to hear this and for another, having experienced the joy of being a true Christian, I wanted to go home and win my friends to Christ and get them out of the "bad" life-style in which they were living.

This is how it went for me. I went into the air force but was soon discharged and returned home. I didn't go to any school afterward. Let me tell you, for a few months I stayed straight. I read my Bible, went to church, and tried very hard. At the time I felt I was doing pretty well, but as time went on, my Bible reading and churchgoing decreased because I didn't associate with Christians, I associated with my old "friends." One day I decided to buy a pack of cigarettes to see how they would affect me. At first smoking was difficult, but soon I found it easier and kept on. A couple of weeks later I had my first drink and eventually ended up getting drunk every week. Then I started smoking marijuana and doing other drugs.

Needless to say, the advice I heard for years was indeed *very true.* I found myself stealing, lying, and worse off than

I was before ever going to the Home. If you could have seen me one month ago, you would understand how badly drugs were controlling me. I cannot stress enough the importance of continuing the life-style you are in now. I am twenty-two and see things very differently from when I graduated at seventeen. You will be easy prey for Satan. Please don't find out the terrible way I have, because it hurts like nothing you've ever experienced. The Bible says that when a Christian gets out of fellowship with God, he is worse off than before giving his life to Christ (2 Peter 2:20, 21). Brother, I can vouch for that with all my heart; it's true in every sense of the matter.

Very fortunately, God has given me another chance to get right with Him. I'm in another home similar to the PAYH except it's a drug rehabilitation center. I'm on probation and cannot believe the mess I have gotten into. God is wonderful, and if you fully trust Him and do your best, you can bet your bottom dollar that He will guide you. Proverbs 3:5 is the best passage that comes to mind. Please continue to grow and mature in Christ and don't fall like I have, for now I'm starting over again at a deeper, lower level. Listen to the staff; they are there to help you and the program has years of experience. Guys have gone both ways—up or down, and it hurts too much to go down. Please continue to live for Jesus, and your life will be so much better. I could kick myself in my tail forever for falling like I have, but as I said, the Lord is giving me one more chance, and I'm going to do what is necessary to accomplish my goals and dreams. Just remember, this is no lecture or false words; it's the truth, and it hurts to learn this way. I'm praying for you, so please include me in your prayers. Thank you.

In Christ's love,
Damon

Another grateful graduate who has kept in touch with us is Stuart, who came to the PAYH in 1987 when he was seventeen "because of my failure to function in society," as he puts it. Stuart began to experiment with alcohol at the age of thirteen and was using marijuana and skipping school a year later. By age sixteen, he was in a drug rehabilitation center. He hated it and ran away on several occasions, only to be returned by police each time. The last time Stuart ran away he broke into a house and the trunk of a car and stole almost six hundred dollars in cash. Soon he found himself detained in the Youth Development Center in Milledgeville, Georgia. "My first night there was the lowest 'down' in my life. I cried and had terrible thoughts," he says. "I prayed, but it was in a very selfish way. I did not know what having a personal relationship with the Lord meant." A preacher came to the detention center and Stuart made a profession of faith in Christ, after which "things improved and I felt a constant peace," Stuart recalls.

Not long afterward, authorities screened him and suggested that he become one of our boys.

"During my first seven or eight months at the Home, everything I did was sneaky, mischievous, rebellious, and plain-out wrong. I almost got expelled," Stuart says. Then finally:

> I recommitted my life to Jesus Christ. I still had struggles, but I knew the Lord was on my side. I began to make closer relationships with the people at the Home. The PAYH became more like my home and family instead of a place I had to go because I was in trouble. I mistrusted adults until I realized that God had supernaturally allowed Glenda Anderson to be like a mother to me. I could talk to her about anything. She was always there for me, taking care of my every need. Because she loved me so much, I slowly began trusting her and, in turn, trusting other adults.

I started to enjoy being at the PAYH. I became a leader and was nurtured by the staff. I received my high school diploma while there. I would still be in tenth grade today if it wasn't for the Andersons' ministry. The Home has blessed me in countless ways. I really believe I would be dead or living on the streets today if I had not come to the Youth Home and received the love and help that was so graciously given to me.

While with us, Stuart regained an interest in sports and started running, placing in eight of nine road races he entered. He received a partial track-and-field/cross-country scholarship to Liberty University. He reports that he is "still growing spiritually and continuing to live by the same virtues I had when I was at the Home. The discipline I received at the PAYH has prepared me 'soooo' much for college, for my running, and for life."

Stan came to the Youth Home in 1966 when he was "at the age either to be 'someone' or a nobody," as he describes it. "I was at a turning point. My parents had divorced when I was six years old." He was with us until he graduated in 1970 from Vidalia High School, where he played football.

Stan says that while at the Youth Home:

I learned respect for myself and others, discipline, and the meaning of "family." I grew academically, physically, morally, and, most important, I learned not to give up because I was led to believe I could accomplish anything if I worked for it. Through Paul, Glenda, and all the people involved with the PAYH (especially Mr. Tommie Q. Vann and Mr. Gerry Achenbach), I learned to cope with life and how to accomplish my goals. I experienced success through faith and hard work. To sum it up, I owe everything I am and have to Paul and Glenda. I know "whose name is on the sign."

Stan went on to South Georgia College for two years and then got a good job with a firm with which he has continued to work. He lives in Atlanta with his wife, Debbie, and their two children. Stan has served two terms as president of the Oregon Park Baseball Association, which involves approximately eight hundred children. "I am by no means financially 'rich,' but I am 'rich' in my family and friends," Stan says. "Through Paul and Glenda, I have learned that I can achieve anything."

Raymond is a graduate who stands out in my memory for several reasons, particularly since he came to us in 1982 during the period when we both were requiring dialysis treatments. In time, we arranged for him to have a kidney transplant. (Until the early eighties, when we accepted Raymond as a member of our family, good health had been a prerequisite to Youth Home admission. However, God made it clear to us that He wanted Raymond entrusted to our care.)

Raymond came to the PAYH because he was "having a lot of family problems and had quit school," as he tells it. Because I was personally experiencing the devastation of hemodialysis, we knew how traumatic it was for Raymond not to have family support and care. He was with us for six and a half years and says, "They helped me graduate from high school, save money to buy a car, and reunited my mother and me. I am very thankful for their concern for my health; they made sure I had the right foods to eat and that I took my medicine. While I was at the Home, I came to know Jesus Christ as my personal Savior." Today, Raymond works in the health-care field and as a security guard on our campus.

As I have suffered through numerous health difficulties, one of the important truths that has become a reality is Romans 8:28: "And we know that all things work together for good to them that love God, to them who are the called according to his purpose." Our eyes need to be set toward how God will show us that blessings will blossom from the ashes of burdens. Raymond is a manifestation of this biblical principle.

Marshall Gomez, who came to us in 1967 as a neglected boy of thirteen, lives in the Vidalia area and reports weekly to the Youth Home to do volunteer work "with the hope that I can return a degree of what was given to me," he says. Gomez recalls that his mother could not control him, and he became a ward of the juvenile courts. I interviewed Marshall in 1967 while he was in the Clayton County juvenile detention center in Jonesboro, Georgia, and told him that, if he was willing to accept the terms of his new home, he could come to live with us.

Marshall remembers:

> While at the Home, I was taught the values of a Christian family and the responsibility each family member has toward the others. In having from twelve to nineteen brothers at any given time, I learned how to work and get along with other people. The Home taught me the importance of having God first in my life, and I was also prepared mentally and physically to compete in life. I was taught how to study. I was required to maintain passing school grades or I was restricted. Physically, we played and competed against each other in team sports. I also participated in individual sports, which taught me how to compete against myself. I learned how to set goals and reach them as a team member and as an individual.

Marshall has been married since the early 1970s and has two children. He and his wife, Carolyn, are active members of their local church. He says that "I still consider the PAYH my home and Paul and Glenda my parents," and we certainly regard him as one of our sons.

Donnell Brown, one of the girls who came to us when we began our ministry in 1963, regularly keeps in touch. She and her husband, Danny, and their son, Russell Edward (I was honored that he was given my middle name), live in Milledgeville, where she is employed at Central State Hospital. Donnell received a B.S. degree in biology from Georgia College in Milledgeville, and in 1978, while working at CSH, earned her M.S. in biology. She soon was transferred to the research department of the hospital, became certified as a clinical laboratory specialist in cytogenetics and as a medical technologist, and today has the title Laboratory Scientist, Senior, in the Clinical Laboratory, Medical Surgical Division of CSH.

Donnell says:

The PAYH has been home to me since 1963. No words could ever express what Paul and Glenda and the PAYH family have meant and will always mean to me. I became a member of the family a month before my sixteenth birthday. Both of my parents had been hospitalized for mental problems.

Through their personal example, Paul and Glenda taught me the love of Jesus Christ, which has sustained me through the years. This is the most important lesson they taught me. The greatest gift they gave me was themselves. Under their love and guidance, I blossomed from a frightened, shy, and lonely teenager into a responsible and caring adult. By encouraging me to get a job in a local department store, they helped me learn to meet people. I learned to manage money and was required to do household chores such as cooking and cleaning, which prepared me to become a wife and mother.

Paul and Glenda taught me to take pride in my personal appearance, and the value of education was stressed. In summary, they taught me all the skills needed to become a productive adult, a wife, a mother, and a good citizen.

Margie Young, a teenager with a need for love and guidance, came to live at the PAYH in the mid-1960s when her father brought his family to Vidalia from North Carolina. When the Youngs arrived, the house they were to occupy was not ready, and Margie ended up living with Glenda and me in the Big House. It was to have been a temporary arrangement, but she continued to live with us even after her family returned to North Carolina about a year later. "Had I not remained with the Andersons, I would not have completed college," Margie says. "But with their help and love, I graduated magna cum laude from Brewton Parker Junior College and then went on to Georgia Southern to obtain my degree in social work."

Margie has been employed by the Georgia Department of Family and Children Services since 1969, first as a caseworker and more recently as a consultant at the state office in Atlanta. "I know without Paul and Glenda's love and support, I would not have accomplished what I have with my life," she declares. "When there have been trying times in my life, I have returned to the Home to be renewed. I have always left strengthened anew and ready to face the challenge ahead. I thank God that the house was not ready when we moved to Vidalia, making it possible for me to live with the Andersons."

Eddie Burris, who has been mentioned in earlier chapters, is a vital member of our staff now, along with his wife, Betty. In 1964, we welcomed Eddie, who had been reared by his grandparents. Following Eddie's grandfather's death, his grandmother's health began to fail. That was when he joined our family. He responded positively, became a solid Christian as well as a real physical specimen, largely as a result of weightlifting, and was named an All State football player while attending Vidalia High School. Eddie has always shown his appreciation. "I do not know and would hate to think about what might have happened to me if the Andersons had not been there when I needed them," he says.

Glenda and I are grateful for the role God has allowed us to have in Eddie's life, and we are also immeasurably thankful to our heavenly Father for all that Eddie and his family mean to us personally as well as to everyone else at the PAYH. Eddie is truly like our son. In fact, because of my immobility, I do not know how I would function without his assistance.

Chuck, who began using drugs at the age of ten, is another person who says if it were not for the PAYH "there is no telling where I would be today." He gives special credit to Truett Andrew, saying he "would not have been able to join the United States Air Force if Mrs. Andrew had not helped me graduate from high school." Chuck served five years in the air force and leaned heavily on the self-discipline and physical conditioning he received at the Youth Home. He says that "the daily Bible study and Bible verses we memorized helped me through troubled times."

Tim Cunningham came to the Home in the summer of 1970 when he was twelve and had nowhere to turn. He had been in a foster home for more than a year but had not adjusted to it. He writes, "Being in the Home taught me most of what has helped me succeed throughout my life, and I thank God every day for having had the chance to grow up there." Tim, who remained with us until he graduated from high school in 1976, says he appreciates having learned "the love and charity that are essential in dealing with other people," plus "self-discipline that is so necessary to have a successful career," all of which enabled him to complete a hitch in the army, part of which he served as a recruiter. He writes that he has been happily married for over thirteen years and has a beautiful three-year-old daughter. Tim recently completed his first two years of college with honors, and "this was possible, in part," he attests, "because I was required to study while at the Youth Home."

It was heartwarming to those of us on the staff to read Tim's closing words: "I have no doubt that I can meet all of life's challenges through Jesus Christ and my family support at the Paul Anderson Youth Home."

Matthew says he gladly chose the Youth Home over juvenile jail and its twelve-foot-high fences with razor wire on top of them. After six years in the air force, where he was an honor student in electronics, Matthew began work with a computer company in Atlanta and today is the senior field engineer for the firm. He credits all of us, especially Eddie and Betty Burris, for helping him turn his life around. He says that after leaving the Home he "came to respect and love my stepfather, whom I once hated and mistrusted; I found him to be one of the wisest men I knew."

Then there is Bill, who says:

> I developed from a scared, skinny boy into a confident, strong young man. I was not prepared to face the world after graduation. I was afraid. I finally decided I didn't have all the answers and called upon Christ for direction. I now have a great family, consisting of my wife, Marsha, and our children, Jenny and Bill. My present job is with Pratt & Whitney Aircraft, where I have had many ideas imple-

mented into their manufacturing processes—two for which I received awards.

Another alumnus heading in the right direction is Jim, a high school dropout hooked on drugs who came to us in November 1987 "without the slightest idea of what life was all about," as he puts it. He is presently attending North Georgia College and has a 3.87 cumulative grade-point average. Jim says:

> This is an absolute miracle in light of the fact that less than two years ago I had dropped out of school after completing only the ninth grade. I am extremely thankful for what God has done for me, and I take a great deal of pride in the fact that the Paul Anderson Youth Home was very instrumental in the changes that have been made in my life.

Wayne is another graduate I want to mention. His story was featured in the March 10, 1990, issue of the *Augusta Chronicle*. At age nineteen, he was a high school dropout sharing cramped quarters with a convicted murderer and six other prisoners. He was quoted as saying that his problems began six years before when his father died, leaving his mother and him to fend for themselves.

"Life sort of went downhill from there. I just ran around town to hang out with my friends," Wayne said. "I turned to drugs to get away from it all."

His mother contacted the PAYH while he was facing a court hearing after selling drugs to an undercover officer, and he came for a stay of thirteen months with us. "It turned me around," Wayne told *Chronicle* staff writer Cathy Geyso. "At first it was like, 'What in the world am I doing here? I don't want to stay here.' But after a while, it became home."

The feature article described Wayne following his graduation from the PAYH as "a clean-cut young man with a bright smile and a military-style haircut," radiating "good health" and talking about "embarking on a career in the culinary arts."

My list of grateful graduates seems endless, and much as the writer of the Epistle to the Hebrews wrote in chapter 11, verse 32, what more shall I say, for time and space fail me. I could list many more graduates, all of whom have continued to keep in touch and express their appreciation for our helping prepare them to go out into the world and become responsible citizens. But appreciation doesn't end with our graduates—Glenda and I are also extremely grateful that God has placed us in a ministry where we have the joy and privilege of being a part of so many precious young lives. What a thrill and adventure it has been!

18
A Closing Challenge

We all have our various talents, and each and every one of us, after discovering his or her individual gifts, should develop them. I challenge you to do this: Cultivate to the ultimate degree the particular talents our heavenly Father has entrusted to you.

I challenge you not to be an individual who becomes so tied up with your own personal field and endeavors that you neglect to recognize the importance of what others have and how they develop their gifts and contribute to mankind. No matter what you have and what you accomplish within your own life, do not build a circle of friends and acquaintances in one dimension. Constantly expand your perimeters. Be interested in others and their contributions.

As we develop our assets and respect those of others, we should never be afraid to venture out in exploration, attempting to discover latent talents that have not presented themselves. After a while, though, surely any person knows his limitations and his strengths. Seeing strong talents possessed by others, we must also realize that their contributions will enhance and amplify what we are personally producing.

We can't do everything ourselves. To give an example, I once knew a man who had an unusual mind. He could solve almost any problem when a need presented itself. Basically he was an inventor. When he saw something that was not working properly, or if there was a need, he could come up with a unique and useful solution to fill that void. Unfortunately, he not only wanted to create new products and ideas but he also would constantly side-track himself into the field of manufacturing many of these tangible objects. He did not have the talents required of a manufacturer or a leader of people. When he tried to produce products that he had invented, he failed. Tragically, this man did not recognize his limitations. He should have allowed others to manufacture the goods he invented. This would have left him free to discover additional products and conveniences that would have benefited others as well as providing financial gain for himself.

Everywhere we look, we see specialists. When you hear the music of a fine instrument, do you appreciate only the talent of the musician? Do not forget that someone designed the instrument and someone else manufactured it. The same is true with all institutions and everything else developed by man. First, these many talents were distributed by God, and each person separately developed his own gift, which made a contribution to society. I am not saying we should minimize ourselves by merely accepting the fact that we have only one role in a culture. What we have as individuals must be considered by us the most important talent of all. There was once an old country-and-western song that said something like, "Do what you do do well, boy." It can't be said better, and I challenge you to do what you do well.

I challenge you not to covet the gifts God has bestowed upon others. An entire lifetime can be wasted if you do not discover your own talents and develop them, and a great contributor to that waste can be the viewing of green fields in the other person's backyard. So many times we have all heard the sour grapes projected by those who say, "If only I had his talents." Countless years can be spent observing others and being jealous of what Our Creator has given them and never looking within to find what God has generously invested in us.

I challenge many of you not to personally accept as a handicap what the world will call a "handicap." Numerous physical or mental problems are given to us just to make us stronger and enable us to give more to the world because we have had the fortitude to overcome them. Some people are born with these personal challenges; others receive them through accidents or illnesses. As I see it, a handicap can be viewed by those of strong character as a challenge or inspiration.

I remember a particular speaking engagement I had at a college. Because of the school schedule and the fact that the auditorium was quite small, I had to do two appearances—one before lunch and the other after the noon meal. As a result, I had the opportunity to have lunch with a portion of the student body in their cafeteria. During this time of eating and fellowshiping, I heard a group of young people enjoying themselves a few tables behind me. There was one female voice full of lively laughter that thrilled me. She sounded as if she were the happiest person on campus.

Finally, without being obvious, I turned to look back and observe the joyous group. As I pinpointed the young lady with the especially happy countenance, I was shocked. She was seated in a wheelchair, had no arms, and only one leg. No one was feeding her. She was actually holding her hamburger with the toes of her only foot! As I observed her, my host told me something about this straight-A student who asked no extra help from anyone. He said she had all of her clothes rigged with strings so that she dressed herself and wholly took care of all her personal needs. I was not about to call her handicapped. She was not asking for my pity or anyone else's. She had accepted her so-called handicap and had become a real winner. I challenge you to do likewise.

I challenge you not to be afraid to be different. I do not mean to be out of the ordinary just for the sake of being that way. I am saying I challenge you not to be afraid to be different if that is what it takes to accomplish the goal God has given you the drive and talents to reach. In my own case, it has meant weighing over three hundred pounds and often nearly four hundred and being viewed as different, to say the very least. I developed the attitude that I was normal and everyone else was a little underweight. I guess this has rubbed off on my family members and even some of my acquaintances. I remember one of the first real observations my daughter made. Paula was about two and a half or three years old when she was looking at some pictures that included men other than her daddy outfitted in athletic garb. Her statement was, "All men have skinny legs but my daddy." This is the way all of us must look at ourselves—as unique creatures whom God has endowed with certain abilities that we are expected to develop to the ultimate degree.

The real challenge I want to leave with you is something I have already touched on several times. I have mentioned that all of our gifts come from God (James 1:17), and surely we should be constantly aware of this. This is not only true of the talents we possess but also of the greatest gift man has ever received. That is the privilege to be a child of the King of the Universe. It is almost beyond imagination to realize that God gave His Son, Jesus Christ, to die for our sins so that we could be His children. We have the opportunity not only to serve Him here on earth but also to spend eternity with Him and our brothers and sisters in Christ. Yes, this ultimate challenge is to accept God's gift, which is the most special blessing we will ever be given, and carry out

His calling here on earth. He has given us our talents, and we should use them for His glory.

Sometimes I hear people talk about what they gave up to go into full-time Christian work and serve God. This goes against my grain. Ever since I gave myself 100 percent to carrying out God's wishes for me, I have realized that I gave up nothing; I am accepting the gift of abundant life that is promised in John 10:10. Indeed, He has given me life and given it to me more abundantly.

What a thrill it has been in times past to be able to stand before five hundred audiences a year and say that the greatest thing in my life is not being an Olympic champion, or being called the World's Strongest Man, but being a Christian. What a privilege this was, what an opportunity.

I am basically a competitor. I want to win, though I am no longer able to perform the feats of strength of years ago or keep up my speaking schedule. The greatest lesson I have learned is that to win I must play on the winning team: the team of Jesus Christ. The other team, of course, is coached by Satan and will look very good at times. It will score points, but in the final quarter and especially when that whistle blows, Satan's team will be decisively defeated.

In this game, there are no spectators on the sidelines and no one in the grandstand. You are either on one side or the other. The attitude "I'm a good person and will never do anyone any harm" will not get it done. Unless you have joined the team of Jesus Christ, accepted Him as your Savior, and are following His guidance, you are playing for Satan. You are a loser. I can speak about this with authority because for many years I was a loser. I was world champion in my chosen sport of weightlifting and was a loser. I was a person of high moral standards and was a loser. I did nothing that would dissipate my body and lived clean in every way, yet I was a loser. I was indeed a loser because I was

playing on Satan's team. I had never joined the winning team.

I found out early that morning in Melbourne, Australia, that though I was called the World's Strongest Man, I could not make it without Jesus Christ. If the World's Strongest Man cannot make it without Him, I don't feel anyone else can. Certainly today, physically limited in my activities, I need Him more than ever.

I challenge you—if you haven't already, join the winning team!

PAUL ANDERSON OFFERS

Because of a growing interest in weightlifting and related subjects and the fact that Paul Anderson has given his life to helping young people and entire families enjoy a more abundant life, he receives many requests for advice from people in all walks of life. Therefore he offers courses, books, films, and cassette tapes on a variety of subjects. To obtain a catalog, write:

Paul Anderson
Paul Anderson Youth Home
P.O. Box 525
Vidalia, GA 30474